Fat Bitch
Copyright © 2018 by Reds Johnson
Interior Design Formatting | Strawberry Publications, LLC

ISBN-13: 978-1722734602
ISBN-10: 1722734604

Dedication

I dedicate this book to my myself. Baby girl, you have been through so much, and somehow you just keep pushing. I know your struggle. I know your pain. I know your hurt. I know how many times you shed tears. I know how many times people judged you without getting to know you. I know how many times you wanted to kill yourself. I know how many times you fought to keep going. I know how many times you were looked at as a liar.

I know how many times you lashed out because you were hurt. I know how many times you were talked about, and no matter how much you wanted to defend yourself you didn't because you knew that no one would listen to you. I know the real you. I know your heart. I know your soul. You have come so far, and I know it may not seem like much, but realize just how great you are.

Appreciate the woman you were before but be in love with the woman you are now. You are a force to be reckoned with. Never let anyone make you feel less than who you are. Never let any man or woman sit high and look down on you. You are destined for greatness. You are beautiful. You are important. You are somebody.

I'm glad you finally found the strength, and the courage to tell your story. You continued to stand firm in your truth. You knew that if you didn't stand for something then you would fall for anything. Regardless, of how many people that dislike you whether it's men, family, ex-friends, readers, authors, and publishers you have been you and nothing but you. I appreciate your strength. I appreciate that no matter how much you wanted to give up you didn't. You may not believe in God 100%, but baby God has a plan for you.

That man ain't letting go of you for some reason, and all you have to do is continue to stay true to who you are, and the things you stand for. Continue to be a wonderful woman, and continue to pray, believe, have Faith and know that through God you can do anything. I love the woman you have become and continue to grow to be an even better woman. I love you girl <3

Acknowledgments

God: Thank you for giving me chance after chance. I know that 98% of the time I doubt you. My Faith and Belief is weak, yet you still show me that you're the one moving mountains in my life. You continue to show me reasons on why I shouldn't give up, and you continue to be there for me even when I don't deserve your love or blessings. I love you.

Maria Ward: Mom, thank you for being there. Thank you for being my strength when I have none. Thank you for being my backbone. Thank you for being my best friend. Thank you for never judging me. Thank you for being the only person who believed in me when myself and no one else did. Thank you for shedding light on my dark situations. Thank you for being a mother first, and a friend second. Thank you for pushing me even when I wanted to throw in the towel. I love you.

CoCo Amoure: Thank you for being the big sister that I never had. Thank you for being such a great support system. Thank you for genuinely caring about me and my wellbeing. Thank you for always being a shoulder for me to cry on. Thank you for riding out with me since day one. Thank you for saying fuck what the industry says, I'm rocking out with this woman regardless. Thank you for welcoming me into your life with open arms. Thank you for keeping the secrets I shared with you close to your heart. Thank you for being you and thank you for allowing me to be me. I love you.

Tia Paul: Thank you for being a down ass friend. You are an amazing woman, sister, and mother. Who would have known a reader would turn into a real friend of mines? Tia you are so awesome. I thank you for being that positive person in my life when things get hard. I thank you for telling me not to respond to the bullshit on Facebook because it's not worth it. I thank you for taking the time out to get to know the real me and nothing but. I thank you for the love, and the support. I love you.

Cynthia Standifur-Curry: Things started out rocky between us, but Queen you showed that you were a true friend. I appreciate you for not stopping until I realized that you weren't out to hurt me. I appreciate your realness. Thank you for love and support. Thank you for letting me know that theirs is no need to respond to the negativity on Facebook. Thank you for staying true when it seemed like everyone was against me. I love you.

Porschee Rogers-Bradley: I have never had a reader share every last post of mines. Crown me as their favorite author and tag me on every drop a name of a dope author post. Thank you so much for being a genuine supporter of mines. Thank you for being real and thank you for not giving a fuck about how people feel about you. The only thing you're worried about is reading good books, and I appreciate that, and I appreciate you. I love you.

Tamara Greene: Thank you for being so supportive, and so down to earth. You saw a light in me that not many readers see or want to see. Thank you for being you and continuing to be a wonderful supporter. I love you.

Sharon P. McKnight: Thank you for the everyday prayers and encouraging words. Thank you for the continuous support. Thank you for Faith you have in me and thank you for believing in me. I love you.

Connect with Author Reds Johnson

Facebook:

Anne Marie Johnson

Back up Facebook Page:

Reds Johnson

Facebook Like Page:

Author Reds Johnson

Twitter:

@ISlayBooks

Instagram:

Reds Johnson

Email:

info@iamredsjohnson.com

Website:

www.iamredsjohnson.com

Other Titles By The Me

Silver Platter Hoe: Everything That Glitters Ain't Gold

Silver Platter Hoe 2: Blood Ain't No Thicker Than Water

Silver Platter Hoe 3: Shit Just Got Real

Silver Platter Hoe 4: Who's The Real H.B.I.C

Silver Platter Hoe 5: Asani's Story

Power Couple: The Desire and Rell Story

Silver Platter Hoe *New Version

Silver Platter Hoe 2 *New Version

Closed Legs Don't Get Fed

Closed Legs Don't Get Fed 2

Harmony and Chaos: A Jersey Love Affair

Harmony and Chaos 2: A Jersey Love Affair

Sincerely, Harmony: The Letter

Harmony and Chaos 3: A Jersey Love Affair

Sincerely, A Real One: Chaos Response

Sincerely, Harmony 2: The Letter

She Don't Deserve The Dick

He Don't Deserve The Pussy

Honey Dipp

Honey Dipp 2: Guy's Revenge

Honey Dipp 3: Secrets

Byron: Life Of A Hustla

Kocaine's Hustle

Dope Dick: The Kane and Dominique story

Never Trust A Ratchet Bitch

Never Trust A Ratchet Bitch 2

A Prostitute's Confessions

A Prostitute's Confessions 2

Thicker Than Most

Hood Vibes

The Bum Bitch Chronicles

Hustla's In Heels

You The King, I'm The Queen: Together We Are Royal

Disclaimer!!!

First off, I'm not writing this story for anyone or anything but ME. I'm not putting my life out there so that people won't have anything to talk about because people are going to talk regardless, and everyone is entitled to feel the way they feel about me. I'm not putting my life out there for a pity party because I don't want one, nor do I need one. I'm not putting my life out there to become famous.

This is my story. My real life story. I'm writing everything from what I remember and how I remember it. You may read certain situations in vivid detail, and other situations won't be. Real names are not mentioned, but these are real life situations. There also won't always be exact dates and time frames. I'm writing my story how I see fit. I'm writing my story to finally get this burden off me and to continue to be at peace and have a peace of mind.

They shamed me on Facebook. They discredited my work, and they talked about my appearance. The readers did what they had to in order to break me, but I'm built Ford tough baby.

-They devil don't know what to do with someone who just won't give up.

Who Am I?

To THE WORLD, I MAY BE NOBODY, BUT THE NAME MY mother gave me is Anne Marie Johnson, along with the nickname Nunni, or Nunnie. I was born in Bridgeton, New Jersey at the Bridgeton Hospital on December 6th, 1993, six days before my mother's birthday. She always told me that I was her early birthday gift because I wasn't supposed to be born yet.

My mother, Maria, went through hell and back when she was pregnant with me. She was being physically and mentally abused by my father. She was depressed and even attempted suicide. She ended up in the hospital while pregnant with me, and I almost died due to coke being in her system.

Now, my mother never did drugs in her life. So, when the nurse came back and asked her how often she did drugs, she was confused.

"Huh?" she asked.

"There was a small strain of cocaine found in your system," the nurse said.

"I've never done drugs in my life. That's impossible. This is impossible," she said.

"Calm down ma'am. We're not going to take your baby. I'm just making you aware of what came back. It can also get in your system from sexual contact," she explained.

My mother was in tears by now. She called my father, distraught.

"Danny, what did you have on your penis? They found coke in my system," she cried.

"Aw, I'm sorry babe. I just put a little coke on my penis. I wanted you to try it," he said in a nonchalant manner.

"What the hell do you mean you wanted me to try it? That could have killed your daughter! Why the hell would you do something like that!"

"Man, get the fuck outta here with all that. It ain't that serious," he responded.

When my mother told me this story, I couldn't believe all that she had endured, just to make sure I came out healthy. She fought to protect me, kept me under her wing, and I never understood it until life got a hold of me.

Growing up, I didn't have it all, and what I mean by that is I didn't have everything handed to me on a silver platter. I watched my mother struggle for years trying to take care of me and my siblings.

You see, I grew up in Cumberland County, and I lived in a small city called Bridgeton. Drugs, killing, fighting, shooting, gangs, sex, you name it, and it happened. My mother kept me and my siblings away from all of that, well at least she tried. On top of being in an abusive relationship, working, and taking care of 4 kids, my mother had her work cut out for her, but she never stopped trying.

What I loved so much about my mother was her strength, and how she never gave up. She didn't go to church, but the faith, hope, and belief she had was unbelievable. My mother truly was a strong woman. There is and there was nothing no one could say about my mother because I knew her pain and I knew her story so, if anyone tried to judge her, I was right there to defend her.

The Woman Who Birthed Me!

THEY SAY AS AN AUTHOR, YOU'RE NOT SUPPOSED TO talk to your readers in your books. Well, this is my book, and I'm going to do what I damn well please. What you all are about to read is the raw, gritty, explicit truth of my life. Now, some of you may read some of the pain and hurt I've been through and ask, where was her mother? A mother should never allow her daughter to go through any of this. So, before that happens, let me start off by saying my mother is my best friend.

She did her very best to raise me, even after all that she's been through. On top of her getting her ass beat by my father, she was also raped and molested by his father, as well as the many guys her mother slept with. My mother, Maria, worked hard, whether it was being a cab driver, delivery driver, a restaurant cook or waitress; she even did hair out of our house.

There were days when she went without eating, just so we could eat. She gave up her entire life for me and my siblings. She dropped out of school, just so she could take care of us because no one would help her. She had no one; her mother, Betty, hated her because she was light skinned, and her father, Lenard, didn't claim her because she was light skinned. Her mother's side of the family did everything in their power to break her.

She was physically abused by her mother, and she was physically abused by my father's father. When she seeked out help, she was looked at as a liar.

And yes, dammit, I believe her! Because she has the scars to prove it! She has a gash in her head from having a hot glass bottle thrown at her. She has burn marks on her stomach and between her legs from having scalded hot water thrown on her. She has a gash on her finger from when my father beat her to a bloody pulp.

My mother always encouraged me, supported me, loved me, nurtured me. Just because she is my best friend didn't mean she wasn't my mother. She was a mother first and my friend second. When it came to the men that used and abused me, she did what a mother was supposed to do. She gave me advice, told me that I didn't deserve to be treated wrong, and she even tried to put hands on a few niggas for me.

My mother's health has been at risk for years. On top of her stress level being up, her having ulcers, a cancerous tumor, and thyroids, she never gave up. She's still fighting to this day because her faith and belief in God is stronger than any health issue or family problem she has.

I watched my father's sisters talk bad about my mother on Facebook. Degrade her for being on welfare, as if they never been on it. They talked about her like a dog, and I never understood why. But, I knew one thing; I always said when I was old enough to defend my mother, I would and that's what I did, which resulted in me almost fighting my aunt Renee.

She took it upon herself to come to our residence and tell me not to disrespect her sister, Mae, who had disrespected my mother the night before. I told her I didn't give a fuck if you was Jesus, you disrespect my mother and I'm on yo ass.

REDS JOHNSON

1

The Molestation:
The Beginning of Life and Confusion

I COULD REMEMBER IT LIKE IT WAS YESTERDAY. MY mother had taken me to the dollar store, and I went into the toy isle. I browsed the toys until I came across a doctor's kit and I just had to have it. Being the spoiled little girl that I was, my mother went ahead and bought it.

I don't remember what happened after we left the store, but I do remember what happened that night. My parents were having sex and my sister wanted to play doctor with me once my parents went to bed. Of course, I agreed. A little girl being able to stay up late and play with toys is the best thing ever, right?

I was in for a rude awakening because when my sister told me to lay down on the bed, she climbed on top of me and lifted up my shirt. I thought this was a part of the game until she placed her mouth on my small breast. She licked on me and sucked on me as she humped me.

I didn't know if what she was doing was wrong or right. I just laid there and let what happened, happen. Moments later, my mother came into the room and she turned on the lights. My sister hopped off me and pretended to be lying down. My mother must have known that something was going on because she asked us what we were doing. My sister responded for us and she said *nothing*.

I assume that my mother knew that it was definitely something going on because my sister got her ass whooped that night, and my mother told me to sleep on the couch.

My father came out of the bedroom and into the living room. I remember his exact words.

"Her dirty ass was touching you?" he said.

"Yea," I responded.

"Yea, well, she just got her ass beat," he told me.

There was nothing else said after that because he turned around, left out of the living room, and went back into his bedroom. The next day, my sister was mad at me. Her words were, "You lied."

From what I could remember, I was confused.

"Lied about what?" I asked.

"You told mom that I was touching you. You agreed to it," she said.

"You did touch me," I replied.

"But, you agreed to it. Now, we can't play anymore because you a snitch."

My feelings were so hurt after she said that. I didn't want to be labeled as a snitch, nor did I want my big sister to stop playing with me. I felt so bad for saying anything. I made a promise that I would never say anything about what happened that night again.

2

Maria

I NEVER SAW MY FATHER BEAT ON MY MOTHER THIS night, but I knew that he did because she was crying and terrified out of her mind. I remember her trying to put my shoes on when he came storming down the hallway yelling in her face. She was sitting on the couch trying to put my shoes on, but I guess because she was so distraught, she couldn't get them on.

I wasn't too sure about what happened but, for some reason, my father went back into the bedroom, and the next thing I knew was my mother picked me up and ran out of the apartment. She ran and hid on the side of a car. My father came outside, stood on the porch looking back and forth, and we sat crouched down until he went back inside. My mother found her way to the nearest bus stop and we went to Millville to her mother's house.

I remember her breaking down to my mother and then, somehow, her and my father got on the phone and they were arguing again.

"I'm tired Danny, I'm tired!" she yelled with tears coming down her face. "How do you think I feel when I hear my baby girl saying she hates me?"

I never recalled me saying I hated my mother, so I couldn't understand why she said that. However, my grandmother looked over at me with hate in her eyes.

"If I ever hear you say you hate your mother around me, I'ma bust ya damn mouth open."

I was young, so I didn't respond. But, as I got older and my mother told me her story, I didn't understand why my grandmother was so worried about me saying I hated my mother, when she was the one that despised her all along.

3

Linette and Jimmy

WHEN MY SISTER LINETTE SAID THAT WE COULDN'T PLAY anymore, she meant that. Because now the target was my brother. I remember coming out of the room I shared with my sister Linette and watching her run down the hallway with a tape in her hand.

"What you doing?" I asked.

"Nothing snitch," she said to me.

"Tell me what yawl doing?" I said while running behind her into the living room.

I watched my sister get on her knees and bob her head back and forth. I thought she had her mouth on my brother's penis, but he burst out laughing and she pulled away, revealing that it was a popsicle. Even though she was playing, she still knew what to get down on her knees and do, so it made me wonder just how many times she possibly could have done that foreal.

Jimmy

I was the one that shared a room with everyone, whether it was my oldest sister or my brother. I never had my own room, and it never bothered me, no matter what went on behind closed doors. I remember Jimmy telling me to get up off the bed. I did, and he told me to turn around. I had on a night gown with panties when I stood up and I turned around. He pulled down my panties and bent me over. I wasn't sure what was going on and why he was doing this.

I didn't stop him until my butt started hurting. I stood up and pushed him back. He tried to stick his penis in my butt again, but I told him no and that it hurt. I remember hearing laughter outside of the window. I walked over and saw our next-door neighbors running back and forth playing tag.

"Let's try it again," he said.

My hands were on the windowsill this time and he attempted to do me from behind again. I didn't understand it, or maybe I did. But, one thing I did knew, I was used by my siblings and I didn't realize how much it mentally fucked me up until now.

4

Annemarie

A LOT HAD HAPPENED TO ME BEFORE THE AGE OF NINE
years old. I was sexually abused by my siblings, and
I walked around like nothing happened. However,
those weren't the first times that my siblings had
sexually abused me, and it damn sure wasn't the last.
It kind of explains why I grew to have such a passion
or writing at the age of nine. No matter where I went
or what I was doing, I always made sure to carry
around a black and white fatigue notebook and my
Andy doll that my father had given me.

I would come up with some of the craziest and
funniest stories, and I never could understand why,
not realizing it was because I had a story to tell. A
deep one, a passionate one, and a real one. Now that
I look back at my life, I realize that the little things
that happened to me was preparing me for a lot more

pains that I was about endure. My passion for writing was going to be my way of releasing those pains.

5

Puppy Love

I WAS ELEVEN YEARS OLD WHEN I MET ASHANTI, WHO was my father's childhood friend's son. I also was eleven years old the first time I started sucking dick, and that was my way of keeping Ashanti. He said he didn't like big girls, and that would get him to like me. His sister was a big girl too, and she had a boyfriend. Her advice to me was: *do it, that's how I keep my boyfriend happy.*

I did it and I knew what I was doing was degrading myself. It was like I cared, but I really didn't because I wanted a boyfriend. From the time I was eleven all the way up until I was thirteen years old, I was sucking Ashanti's dick to keep him happy.

I grew to be even more ashamed of what I was doing to keep him happy when one day, I went to school, which was West Avenue at the time, and all of the kids were talking about sex, sucking dick, and eating pussy. I didn't join because I already didn't fit in and because I didn't want anyone to know that I was just a tab bit experienced.

But, me not joining in didn't stop them from knowing, but a boy by that we called Fat Boy blurted out, "Anne suck dick, and I know that for a fact!"

I was shocked that he would announce something like that and, being that I wanted to remain innocent because that was my personal business, I denied it.

"No, I don't," I said.

"Yea, you do. Ashanti told me. He said you suck his dick all the time and that you be bitin' him sometimes," he laughed.

All I could do was put my head down because what he was saying was true. There were times where I bit Ashanti while giving him head because I didn't know what I was doing. I was inexperienced. I was embarrassed to no return, and the sad part about it was me and Ashanti didn't even go to the same school.

So, I dealt with that rumor for a while. I even had the older guys in school coming up to me while in school and asking me if I wanted to suck their dicks in the bathroom. They said that I should be down with it because I was fat, so they were making me look good. Even Ashanti's older brother confronted me one time when I was at their house, and he wanted to know if I was willing to give him a blow job.

I had never shared this bit of information with my family, due to me being too embarrassed, so I dealt with it alone. I was always aware that I was a big girl, but what I didn't know was that being a big girl was going to cause me more hurt than happiness.

6

The Start of My Low Self-Esteem

I WAS THIRTEEN YEARS OLD WHEN I THOUGHT THAT Ashanti had taken my virginity. Hell, he thought so too. I remember it like yesterday. We were sitting on the floor of the living room in my mother's half of double house. My mom had just gone upstairs when Ashanti pulled me on top of him. I had on some booty shorts, and he slid them to the side as he pulled his pants down a little. His dick wasn't even as big as my pinky so, when he put it in, I felt nothing. I did get wet, which was why I thought he took my virginity.

I was on top of him for a few seconds before we heard my mother coming back downstairs. Ashanti ran with the fact that he'd thought he took my virginity for years. I eventually told him that his dick was too small to do any damage or take anyone's virginity.

"I don't care. You a fat ass anyway," he said.

He was mad that I said he had a small dick, but it was true. I wasn't trying to play him at all, but he thought I was.

That wasn't the first time Ashanti had disrespected me. He did me dirty time and time again. He'd done some really grimy things to me and one of them was on his birthday. I didn't have much back then, so I dressed the best I could in pair of blue jeaned capris, a black and yellow shirt and, considering my hair wasn't looking the best, I wore a black and yellow head scarf.

While his party was going on, a few of his school friends asked if I was his girlfriend.

"Nah, I don't date fat girls. That's my sister's friend."

I stood there looking stupid. I mean, what could I say? He was denying me right in front of everybody and my feelings were hurt. He and his friends walked away laughing and clowning me, while I turned and went over to the group of girls that were surrounded in a circle.

The females that were there were Ashanti's friends from school and from his old neighborhood.

One girl in particular kept staring at me, as if she had a problem. I ignored her because I didn't know her from a can of paint and I didn't understand what her problem was. I wasn't trying to turn his party out, so I remained calm.

That same night, Ashanti went to stay at one of his friend's house. As soon as he left, Candice came into the kitchen.

"You know him and that girl go out, right?" she said.

"What girl?"

"That light skinned girl that kept staring at you. They go together. That's why he going over there to stay the night."

I didn't believe Candice because I had found out long ago that she did and said things just to hurt me because she was hurting but, sure enough, when Ashanti came back and I asked him, he confessed.

"Yea, we together. I been broke up with you."

"You know how ignorant that is? Like, when were you going to tell me, and why would you just break up with me for no reason whatsoever?" I asked.

"You fat and you dark skinned. She's skinny and she's light skinned. What I look like having you on my arm when I can have something like her on my arm."

That was the day I became ashamed of my skin color. He put a stain on my heart and on my brain that told me that I would never be beautiful because I wasn't light skinned, also because I was fat.

7

The Fight & The Start To My Anger

I ALREADY DIDN'T REALLY LIKE CANDICE BECAUSE OF her knowing that Ashanti was with other females and then laughing in my face as if she didn't know it. I also wasn't feeling her because she'd embarrassed me in a house full of company saying that it was me that was smelling, knowing it was really her. We were both big girls, but she was bigger than me and she was the type of big girl that tried to outshine and make the next big girl look bad, which resulted in us throwing hands, also known as fighting.

We were practicing a dance for their little sister's birthday party and, all of a sudden, Candice hit me. I didn't know why she hit me, and I didn't care. All I know was I started throwing blows. I was about fourteen at the time and she was seventeen. I was tearing her face up and her brother was sitting on the sideline yelling *"get her Candice!"*

The only thing she was doing was kicking me and that shit hurt. I was already chunky and out of breath because I was trying to get on top of her too so that I could have a better advantage and continue to pound her face in. She clearly wasn't having it because she kept kicking me as hard as she could.

I ended up getting a hold of her hair with my left hand and throwing nothing but quick rights. I wasn't sure how we got separated but we did, and that's when I called my big sister Dani.

"Tell that lil girl to keep her hands off you before I come over there and fuck her up. I'm too grown for this shit and her fat ass is too fat for this shit," Dani said.

"My sister said you better keep ya hands off me before she come over here and fuck you up," I repeated.

Candice never said anything once I told her that. I hung up with my sister, and we waited for my mother to get back, who had just run to the store. When she got back, I told her that me and Candice was fighting, and she was so upset at us both.

"Yawl fighting, and yawl could've fucked up this house. That shit ain't cool and, Nunni, you know better," she said.

She waited for Ashanti's father to come home, who was also Candice's stepfather, to tell him what happened; he was pissed. Candice got beat with a belt, and my mom beat me and I couldn't understand why when I wasn't the one who started it. They made us go in the backyard and clean up, and I barely helped because I didn't feel like I should have, considering it wasn't my fault.

I noticed after that, my anger got worse. I would punch brick walls until my knuckles bled, just because I was so angry at everything and everyone. I didn't feel the pain, not then and not after. I had a dark spirit and a dark soul that had taken over me, and I had no clue that it was going to get worse.

$\mathscr{8}$
The Fight

IN MY HOUSEHOLD, THERE WAS ALWAYS A LOT OF
arguing and physical fighting, whether it was my
parents, me and my siblings, or my siblings and my
parents. This day wasn't no different from any other
day. Linette had a thing for getting a boyfriend and
saying fuck the family, the same as Dani. My mother
had cooked the night before, and Linette and her
boyfriend Armando came to the house to get
something to eat.

For some reason, this day, my father had an
attitude. He and Linette passed words and, the next
thing I knew, he had thrown the plate that Linette
had just fixed in the trash.

"Mom, this nigga just threw my fuckin' plate in
the trash!" Linette came screaming in the living room
where my mother was sitting on the couch.

I was sitting on the floor watching TV but, with all the commotion going, I turned around to figure out what had just happened.

"Nigga, what the fuck you say?" he asked.

Linette turned around and started pointing her finger in our father's face. The next thing I knew, they started fighting, I mean literally fighting like two enemies off the street. My mother jumped up and tried to break it up. Armando was in the middle as well, but I wasn't sure what he was trying to do because in the midst of him breaking it up, he was sneaking in hits on my dad.

"Linette, what the hell is wrong with you? You swinging on ya dad like a nigga of the street."

"Fuck you! You always choose that nigga over us!"

Linette and Armando stormed out of the house, and I was sitting there in awe. That wasn't the first time that I had heard one of my sisters say that my mother chooses my father over us. I didn't quite understand it at first because I didn't see it until I got older.

I didn't know if it was her choosing him over us, but there were more than enough times that we wouldn't have something, and my father would. Things such as, we would have to fight to find something to eat in the fridge, but my father would have takeout. We would have to eat a certain dinner, and my father would have something a little more spectacular. It wasn't right and I would never say it was, but my mother's past explains her every action, and I also didn't know that until I got older.

9

Homeless/Almost Death Experience

THE FIRST TIME I EXPERIENCED BEING HOMELESS WAS when I was fourteen. I remember I was getting tutored because that was one of the times that I had dropped out of school. My tutor was Mrs. King at the time, an elderly lady that had grown to be a friend of the family because she had tutored my brother when he was out of school for almost a year due to his severe asthma, which kept him in and out of the hospital.

I stopped going to school because I was getting bullied. It was overbearing for me, and I had just given up. On this particular day of me getting tutored, everyone was extremely tired. My mother had taken a nap and, when she woke up, she was hungry, so Mrs. King gave her money to go get Chinese food.

"Mrs. King. I have to go take a shower. I can't stay awake," I told her before getting up from the table.

I went upstairs in my bedroom and took out some clothes. I also checked on my turtles, Cheetah and Speedy, that my sister Dani had gotten me just because. I grew to love them, and my favorite animals turned out to be turtles. Once I was finished, I went in the bathroom, turned the water on, and got in.

I hadn't even been in the shower for five minutes before I heard a loud crash. I stood in the shower in a frozen state. I couldn't move. My body and the fear that took over me wouldn't allow me to. I don't know how long I was standing there, but I finally was able to pull the curtain back, and there was a crack in the bathroom wall.

"Nunni! Nunni! Nunni, answer me!" Mrs. King yelled.

I hopped out of the shower and opened the door to see my father limping out of his bedroom. He was covered in white stuff as he held onto the wall and made his way down the stairs. I peeked in his room and saw a huge hole in the ceiling where the chimney had crashed down into his bedroom. My dad was an animal fanatic; he had tarantulas, red devil fish, and scorpions, and all of them but two had died due to the chimney crashing in the bedroom.

The chimney wasn't even an inch from his bed. If it had fell any closer, my father would have been crushed to death.

"My dad almost died. Oh, my God, my dad almost died," I cried as I ran to my bedroom crying.

My dad managed to call my mother and she couldn't believe what she was hearing. When she got back to the house, she ran upstairs and broke down in tears when she saw their room. By this time, I was dressed, and she had called 911. The cops and ambulance arrived, as well as the landlord.

"You guys are going to have to evacuate immediately because from the looks of it, that chimney is going to fall again."

We couldn't stay even if we wanted to because there was carbon dioxide in the house, which was why we was all so tired.

The moment the police officer said that, I took action. I ran into the house, got a few big black trash bags, and started running to each room packing our stuff. I grabbed what I thought everyone needed before grabbing my turtles last.

"Make sure you get your school books!" Mrs. King yelled.

I made sure I threw my school books in the back of a stand, so no one would find them. I didn't appreciate her worrying about some school books, when my dad could have lost his damn life. After I was done in the house, I got in Mrs. King's car, and her fat ass was sitting in there eating a damn egg roll.

"Nah, fuck that! I want my shit!" my father yelled.

I looked out the window as I sat in the backseat watching my father go back and forth with the police, and my mother trying to calm him down. He snatched away from her and got in the car with me. That was the first day I saw my father cry and it broke me something serious.

That same night, we were put in a hotel called the Days Inn at the time. My mother was going over Ashanti's parents' house and I wanted to go with her. I didn't want to be away from her, and she told me I didn't have to. However, the next thing I knew was my aunt Pearl coming to the hotel. I didn't know why she was there, but my mother waited until she got there to tell me that I wasn't going with her.

I got mad at her, and I remember Pearl asking me why I was mad, and I told her.

"I don't want to be away from my mother."

Pearl grabbed me by my arm and put me outside in the cold and shut the hotel door.

"When you get some damn sense, then you come back in?"

My mom didn't do anything to defend me and that pissed me off. After about ten minutes, Pearl finally came back out and asked me was I ready to come in. I didn't say anything, but I did push past her and walk back into the hotel room.

"Nunni, get ya stuff," my mom told me.

"I'm not going nowhere," I said.

The next thing I knew, my mother grabbed me by my shirt and slammed me around. Ashanti's mother Ivy and Pearl had to pull her off me. She ripped my earing out my ear, and all I could do was cry.

"Nunni, you are only thirteen years old. You don't have the right to talk back to your mother or try to fight her."

"SO!" I yelled back.

Ivy slammed the door, and I wanted to hop out that damn truck and kick that bitch in her face. I wasn't trying to fight my mother, but my mother was trying to fight me.

"Nunni, I'm telling you now. You either going to stop crying or I'm leaving ya ass here. I don't want you at my house no way," Pearl said to me.

I didn't stop crying, but I did silence myself. That night, my mother called my sister Linette and told her that Mrs. King was coming to pick us up and take us out to dinner. I didn't give two fucks about dinner or anyone else for that matter. We ended up going to dinner anyway, which wasn't nowhere but Denny's. I was quiet the entire time and made sure my facial expression was cold, just so no one would talk to me.

Living with my aunt turned me into an angry person. She tortured me. Whenever I would try to go to sleep early or go to sleep after I came home from school, she would make me take a cold shower until she thought I had enough. When I was hungry, I couldn't eat until she felt like I was hungry enough, and she had a rule that when she cleaned her kitchen, I couldn't get anything to eat or drink.

I would call my mother every night telling her that I wanted to come live with her in the hotel, which was a rat trap, but I didn't care. Whenever she would want to agree, I would hear my father in the background snapping because he didn't want us there with him. There had been many signs that my father showed me that he didn't care for me, but he was my father so what could I do?

Linette and Dani were living with my aunt as well, and they saw what she was doing to me and not once did they defend me. I was their baby sister and they watched a woman that was supposed to help us torment me. I guess since they were the ones that got to hang out with my aunt, then they didn't care what was happening to me. They didn't care about the many nights I went hungry or the many times she would make me take a cold shower, just because I was tired. They didn't care how she got mad that I was calling my mother at night and, before I knew it, she had taken the phone out of the bedroom I was in.

I went to school and got picked on for stinking, on top of my sister Linette peeing in the bed that my clothes were on, my aunt would take my clothes and my panties, so I was forced to wear the same outfit for a week and sometimes more. My mother didn't know any of the abuse I was enduring, and I didn't tell her because I felt like she wouldn't care because if she did, then she wouldn't have left me with my aunt to begin with.

I was mad at my mother for months. I remember her coming over to pick me and my sisters up because it was Christmas morning and I didn't give two fucks that she had been crying. I was still mad at her for choosing to take my father with her, instead of me. When we got to the Cohansey Hotel and went into the room, there were Christmas presents on the bed.

I remember staying the night with my parents that night and waking up in the middle of the night seeing my mom and dad gone. I panicked a bit because I thought they had left me, but then I heard moans coming from the bathroom. A short while after, my father came out of the bathroom and I caught an instant attitude. I wasn't dumb. I knew they were having sex, and it disgusted me. We were homeless and the only thing that was on their mind was fucking?

A month or so later, my parents had to leave the hotel because the landlord had stopped paying for our stay. My parents ended up living with my other aunt named Gladys. Pearl and Gladys were my father's sisters, and they were both pieces of shit. They disrespected my mom time and time again, and my father sat back and allowed it to happen. Eventually, I went to stay with Gladys as well because Pearl put me out because I missed my bus one day.

I was young, but I knew wrongdoings when I saw them, and they were doing my mother dirty. I got tired of seeing my mother cry, but she really didn't have a choice because we were homeless, and we had nowhere to go. So, I watched her endure the verbal abuse from my aunt Gladys. That was the day I realized my mother was afraid to defend herself and I couldn't understand why, and that was also the day I made a promise to myself that, once I got old enough to defend my mother, I would at all cost.

10

The Start of Internet Dating/ My Mental Break Down

I WAS FOURTEEN YEARS OLD, AND I HAD JUST STARTED the internet dating thing. I made an account on a dating site called Tagged. I put up my best pictures on the site and, before I knew it, my inbox was raining with messages. I received one inbox from a guy named Chazz. He wasn't all that cute but he had really pretty hair, which was why I responded to him at the time.

Chazz: *Wassup boo?*

Me: *Hey*

Chazz: *How old are you? You look young, but that body look older.*

Me: *I'm fourteen about to be fifteen. How old are you?*

Chazz: *I'm nineteen boo, but we can still be friends. I can come pick you up, take you out, and we can hang around ya way until you hit sixteen and then we can make it official.*

It didn't dawn on me that he barely knew me but was willing to come and see me and take me out. I was just happy to attract another guy besides Ashanti. Me and Chazz had been talking for a few months before I told my mother about him, and she wanted to talk to him. The only source of communication me and Chazz had was Tagged and Yahoo messenger. I remember him and my mother's exact conversation.

Chazz: *Can I take care of ya daughter?*

My mother read the messages and she looked surprised. She was well aware that I was fourteen and that Chazz was nineteen, but she supported me and had my back in any and everything. Besides, around this time, I was about to turn fifteen and she didn't mind me having a friend.

Maria: *Of course, just don't hurt my baby or I will hurt you.*

Chazz: *I'll never hurt your daughter. I want to take her out this Friday if that's okay.*

Maria: *That's fine. Just make sure you keep my baby safe.*

Chazz: *You got my word.*

That Friday, I got dressed all pretty, and my sister Linette did my hair in pretty crimps. Once I was ready, my mother walked me down the street to the store where we were supposed to meet at. His car was nowhere in sight, and I assumed he was just running late. There was no way for me to call him because he never gave me his cellphone number. We had only talked on the phone once and he called me private because he said he was using his sisters phone.

"Mom, let's just go," I said.

My mom was persistent. She still looked around to see if she saw his car. I began to walk back home, and I held in my tears. I had been stood up for the very first time. When we got home, my mother was furious. She got on my Yahoo messenger app and wrote Chazz.

The next day, someone called our house phone and my mother picked up the phone. Her mouth had dropped open and, when she hung up, she revealed to me what happened.

"Chazz got shot and he's in the hospital."

I broke down in tears and I did everything in my power to find a ride to Newark. I didn't get a ride, but I did blow Chazz's messenger up until he finally was able to respond. He did, and he told me he was still in the hospital. When I told him that I wanted to visit him, he would always make an excuse and said he couldn't have any visitors. It was just weird to me how he was in the hospital but posting recent pictures of him out and about on Tagged.

I noticed whenever I went on Tagged, the same girl would comment on Chazz's statuses and his pictures. I always questioned him about it, but he said she was just a friend. My gut told me that he was lying, and he was because my mother found out that she was his wife and that his entire life had been a lie. He was really thirty-two years old, and I wasn't the only young girl that he had been dealing with or wanting to deal with.

When I confronted Chazz once again, he said I was tripping and that he wasn't married because he was only nineteen years old. He ended up telling me he would see me soon, and that made me happy. I told him that my birthday was coming up and could he pay for my party.

"Give me a price baby and I got you."

That same night I was on Tagged, a guy hit me up, and we chatted a few. He asked me for my number, and I told him that I had a boyfriend. He let me know that there wasn't a harm with having friends, and my stupid ass gave him my number. The next thing I knew, Chazz was blowing up my messenger telling me that I was a hoe and that he would never give me a dime. I didn't understand what he was talking about, but I found out when I went back on Tagged and saw that the same guy that messaged me had confessed to being Chazz's best friend and that him hitting me up was just a set up.

Before I even had a chance to respond, the guy had deleted his profile. Everything happened too fast for me to even process exactly how did I end up in such a situation. Chazz didn't even break up with me for an hour before he put a picture up of him and the same girl that he denied being with in the first place, and the caption read *wifey.*

I was in tears when I told my mother what happened. I felt so stupid because Chazz was the very first dude that I had sent nude photos to.

"Baby, you did nothing wrong. That was just his way of getting rid of you because you kept nagging at him about the truth. He needed a way to get rid of you, and his homeboy hitting you up and them setting you up was the way."

11

Almost Raped

I DIDN'T GET TO HANG OUT WITH MY SISTERS AS MUCH so, when my sister Linette asked me did I want to go to our cousin Aaron's house to hang out, I jumped for joy. We both had on matching outfits and couldn't no one tell me shit. We ended up drinking and having fun and, while Linette was with her boyfriend, I was right under her.

"Girl, go over there somewhere," she said.

Aaron pulled me close to him and tried to kiss me. I pushed him away because he was my cousin and that's just not how I got down. Not only that, but I was fourteen and he was a grown ass man trying to kiss on me. When I pushed him back, he groped me between my legs and grabbed my pussy.

"Stop!" I said.

"Nunni, chill out and stop being so corny," Linette said.

"You don't wanna have sex with me?" he asked.

"No, I don't," I told him.

Linette and her boyfriend went into the bedroom, leaving me and Aaron along.

"Why you don't wanna have sex with me?" he asked.

"Because that's nasty," I told him.

"No, it's not. But, we gonna have sex. I'm going to get some condoms. I'll be back," he said and got up and left.

I sat there scared shitless. I couldn't go to my sister because she didn't care, and I couldn't walk home by myself because it was dark outside. It seemed like God was with me that night because I heard banging on the door. I jumped, and my sister ran out of the bedroom. She went to the door and opened it, and it was my mother.

"Where is Nunni?" she asked, and she was out of breath.

"I'm right here mom," I said.

"Let's go right now," she demanded.

"What's wrong?" Linette asked.

"I don't like the feeling I got, so I came to get her now let's go Nunni," she said.

I got up and put my jacket on and left out of the house. My mom grabbed my hand and we started to walk home. I looked up at her, and it was like she was reading my mind on what I wanted to ask because she answered before I could even say anything.

"Mommy saw something that she didn't like, and I had to come get you. I walked my fat ass down here as fast as I could, and I wasn't going to stop until I got to you," she told me.

12

Reconnection

IT WAS MY LAST FEW MONTHS OF BEING FOURTEEN WHEN I finally reconnected with my half-sister Quana, who was just nine months older than me. We lost touch when we were nine years old, due to her family not liking my mother. One day her grandfather came to pick her up so that she could stay the night with them, and they never brought her back.

Finally, I had the chance to meet her and, when I did, I didn't recognize her. She had on a mini, cut-up jean skirt with thong panties and a black shirt that barely fit, big blonde braids in her hair with tons of make up on.

Both myself and my mother looked at each other in disbelief. When I saw Quana again, she pulled out the cellphone that my mom had given me and threw it at me.

"Here, this don't work."

I looked at her and then at the phone. "You stole my phone?"

"Yea. Because I needed a phone," she said.

I didn't hesitate to tell my parents, but it was like it was her word against mines. They didn't believe me. I mean, why would they? A girl with a sweet and innocent voice would never do such thing, right? That was the first time Quana had stolen from our house and it wasn't the last.

13

The Fight

QUANA HAD TAKEN ME THROUGH HELL AND BACK. ALL she did was torment me and lie on me. She made my life miserable in school. Talked about me so bad, and even went out with and fucked the boy that she knew I had a huge crush on.

There had been so many times that I had try to sit down and talk to her to just see why? Why are you so spiteful, vindictive, and hateful?

"What is your beef with me? Every time I look you doing some reckless shit," I asked once.

"I don't know what you're talking about," she smiled.

Quana always had a conniving look to her. She always gave this evil smile like she knew what she was doing, but she gave no fucks. She didn't care what she did and who she hurt in the process of her doing so.

It had gotten so bad that I was starting to stress in school. My cousin Nyemah, who was my cousin by marriage, was sick and tired of seeing me stress, and she confronted Quana. I had no idea that she had said anything to her until Quana came to my classroom. I was at an afterschool program and shit ended up getting heated.

"You need to check ya cousin. Tell her don't be confrontin' me about anything," Quana said.

"I'm right here. Say it to me!" Nyemah yelled.

"Girl bye!" Quana waved her off.

It was then that I knew that Quana was all bark and no bite. Nyemah had confronted her about all the bullshit she had been doing to me and my family, and Quana just couldn't take someone on the outside knowing the truth or at least wanting the truth.

"What happened?" I asked.

"I got tired of seeing you hurting, so I asked the bitch what her problem was. She walked away without saying anything, and I followed her. That bitch is the devil. I know bitches like her!" Nyemah yelled.

At this time, we were only in the seventh grade. So, for Nyemah to feel so strongly about the situation made me feel good. I was happy that someone else could see what I was seeing because I didn't have anyone backing me besides Linette and, considering me and her was the loudest ones, no one listened.

14

Harsh Words

WHEN IT CAME TO BOYS, QUANA TOOK ME THROUGH IT. She made sure she stepped in when any guy took any sort of liking to me. Not only that, but she would purposely hook me up with someone and, then afterwards, she'll tell them what I really looked like. Back then, we only had a house phone. I wasn't allowed to have a cellphone, and I wasn't allowed to be on the internet either. So, no one but her knew what I looked like.

"Did you tell white Adam that I was fat, ugly, and I wore glasses?" I asked.

"Yea."

"Why?"

It was bad enough that I was the only sibling that was bigger, and to know that my own blood sister would make me look bad to a guy, knowing that guys didn't like me as it was, hurt me a great deal.

"Because I liked him, and I felt like you knew it."

White Adam was a guy that lived in Vineland, New Jersey. Quana knew him first but, because he was white, she didn't want him. Me, personally, I didn't do white guys but, at the time, I didn't see anything wrong with talking to someone over the phone. I never knew that Quana liked white Adam. Again, she told me she didn't like him because he was white. I could never see myself dating outside my race but having a friend that was white didn't hurt me none, which was why I was talking to him.

"Nobody knew you liked him and, furthermore, you talked to Ashanti. Knowing that he was my on and off again boyfriend for the last couple of years," I told her.

"Because he liked me back. He said he never liked you because you was fat. I told you when I came down here that I was gonna get him, and I did."

I didn't say anything back. I couldn't say anything back. All I knew was that my anger for her was building up and, pretty soon, I was going to snap on her.

15

The Fight

QUANA HAD DONE A LOT AND SHE HAD ONLY BEEN living with us for a couple years. During this time, my mother had almost been arrested because Quana told the school that my mother was abusing her and wasn't feeding her. She would bleach my clothes, spit in our food, put boogies on my mother's wash cloth, and even went as far as to putting alcohol in my mother's bodywash, which resulted in her being rushed to the hospital.

Even after all of this, my mother still gave her the benefit of the doubt, and I remember the night that Linette had just had about enough of the bullshit.

"That girl is fake, and she's a trouble maker. Every time I look, Nunni is getting in trouble for some shit Quana did. Sister or not, I don't like the bitch."

"Linette, watch ya mouth in my house," Maria told her.

"I'm not watching shit. Nunni is going through hell and no one cares. The only thing yawl doing is punishing Nunni, while Quana sit back and smile."

"Linette, I know you don't like me! You always got something smart to say to me!" Quana yelled.

Everyone was shocked because the quiet and innocent Quana had finally made some sort of outburst. I looked at Quana, who was sitting across the table from me, and then I looked back at Linette.

"Um, do you wanna fight?" Linette asked.

Linette was just waiting for any reason to pop on Quana because she was tired of her, and so was I. She had done so much wrong and it was time for her to pay the price, and she was damn near about to because before I knew it, Linette was charging across the table swinging at Quana, and my mother grabbed her by her hair and pulled her back.

I took it upon myself to hop up and swing on Quana. My finger was broken, but that didn't stop me from trying to beat her ass, and I know people are reading this like how can yawl try and jump yawl sister? Jumping her wasn't the plan, but Quana had did too much shit and, once I saw that Linette wasn't for it, I finally felt like I could let my guard down and finally take action because I was tired.

After it was all said and done, Linette was kicked out and I was put on punishment so, once again, Quana had a reason to be pleased.

16

The Fight

I HAD FINALLY HAD ENOUGH OF QUANA WHEN SHE HAD a talk with my mother about how I was treating her. Really? How I was treating her? But, of course, my mother believed her every word. I remember this night like it happened last night, and my mother came upstairs to talk to me about talking to her.

"Nunni, you really need to give that girl a chance," she said.

"Are you serious?" I asked.

"Yes, I'm very serious. I'm about to go to the store, and I want yawl to talk and, if you don't, you will be grounded. Mark my words."

I was pissed, but I didn't want to be ground, so I went downstairs to talk to her. Only, I didn't say anything, I let her do the talking first.

"What's your problem with me?" she started.

"You just fake, and you bleached my clothes," I told her.

"You don't have no proof that I bleached your clothes," she smiled.

I wasn't for any of the dumb shit she was on, so I cut the conversation short because I could feel myself getting upset.

"I'm done talking."

"No, you're not. You got no choice but to sit here because your mom said you have to talk to me and, if you don't, you're on punishment. So, do you really want me to tell her that you didn't talk to me?" she smiled again.

I remained quiet, but my blood was boiling by now.

"You gonna always be a nobody. You don't go to school. No boys like you, and you're fat. That's why I slept with Ashanti. He didn't want your fat ass. I look better than you and I'm better than you, and I'm keep doing what I'm doing because ain't nobody gonna believe you and, hell yea, I bleached your clothes," she said.

By now, my mother was back, and she had Linette with her. She came in the house smiling with bags in her hand.

"Did yawl talk?" she asked.

"Yea, but Nunni ain't tryna hear anything I'm saying. She was real ignorant to me when you left," Quana said.

My mom turned to me and snatched my mp3 player out of my hand. "I guess you thought I was playing. You're grounded."

"I'm grounded, but this bitch just said all that shit to me? Get the fuck outta here!" I snapped.

Linette was shocked by my outburst because that wasn't me unless somebody pushed me to the edge, and she looked at Quana, ready to knock her head off.

"What did she say Nunni?" my mom asked.

"She talking about how she bleached my clothes and calling me fat and all this."

My mom looked over at Quana, who had a smirk on her face.

"I didn't say anything like that Maria," she lied.

The next thing I knew, I had flipped the table over on her and tried to run around the table to grab her. I don't know how my mother got to me, but she grabbed me and slammed me up against the wall. I grabbed all types of knick-knacks that was on a stand beside me and threw them at her. I wanted at least one of them to crack her in her damn head. I was still acting like an animal trying to get at her and, at first, she acted like she wanted to fight but, once she saw that I was serious and that she had gotten me out of character, she calmed down.

However, Linette wasn't having that. She squared up with Quana and punched her dead in her face, and Quana did nothing but sit there. When I saw that, I dipped my mother like I was on a football field, and I was seconds away from grabbing Quana when Jimmy came out of nowhere and pushed me in my chest so that I wouldn't grab her.

Once all of my rage and anger stopped, I was in full blown tears screaming how I was tired of her and how I hated the family because no one believed me about the stuff she was doing to me and, no matter how hurt I was at that moment, that still didn't stop the cops from being called on me.

17

Marcus

I DROPPED OUT OF SCHOOL AT THE AGE OF FIFTEEN years old, due to me getting severely bullied by students and teachers because of my weight and my skin color. Tutoring wasn't an option because people claimed they feared me so much and I gave off a dark energy, so I just said fuck school altogether. I felt like I wanted to be somebody, but life was like nah bitch, you ain't going to be shit but who you are already and that's a nobody.

Now, I wasn't dumb. When I was going to school, I got nothing but A's and B's. I was either hitting the honor roll or principal's list, and I even got chosen to go to the school of gifted and talented, but I couldn't handle that either because my weight was the main focus.

So, I dropped out and did nothing but sleep, eat, and be on the internet. I even went as far as to doing chatline dating, where I met a dude named Marcus. Marcus had my young, dumb ass stuck on stupid. He had me calling females that had said he'd gotten them pregnant and, when I didn't do what he asked, he would get so angry with me.

"You a stupid dumb bitch. I can't wait until the day you die. You couldn't even do one simple thing that I asked you, dumb bitch."

I didn't leave him. I dealt with the things he said to me. I was young and I was dumb, at least that's what was instilled in my mind. No matter how much verbal abuse Marcus had given me, I still stuck around. No, we never met and, after seven months of us dealing with each other, he had stopped talking to me out of nowhere. He'd changed every number I had for him and, when I finally did remember that I had his aunt's phone number, she revealed to me that her nephew was gay.

***

Marcus

Marcus wasn't the only guy that I had met off the chatline. I met a guy named AJ who lived in New York. AJ wanted to be a rapper and I supported him but, when I told him I wanted to be an author, he would just laugh.

"You didn't even finish school. How you gonna be an author?" he asked.

He was right; how could I be an author when I didn't finish school? I allowed him to put me in a sunken place when I shouldn't have. I never met AJ, but he had a mental hold on me. I knew he was dealing with other women, but I stayed. I felt like, since I couldn't please him, he had to get it from somewhere.

AJ even went as far as to trying to talk to Linette, and she entertained it for a while until she finally decided to block him from Facebook after he had kicked my back in. That was another reason I hated Linette. She knew what I had been through with men and she just didn't care. It was like she wanted me to hurt more than I already was.

18

Did God Love Me or Did He Not

I WAS THROUGH WITH LIFE BY NOW. NOT THAT I HADN'T been through with life before, but I was damn sure through with it now. Everything seemed to just be crumbling right before my eyes. I mean, nothing, not a damn thing was going right. I was cutting myself more, and I had even tried to overdose on pills. Nothing worked, and I couldn't understand why. Why was it so hard for me to die? I wanted to die. I didn't want to live anymore, so why the fuck wouldn't God allow it?

Why did he keep me here to just be hurt, tormented, used, and abused by people? Why did I have to constantly go through the bullshit that I was going through? I wasn't shit, and I knew I was never going to be shit so, why was I still breathing? Why didn't he just allow me to kill myself like the many time I wanted to? I couldn't understand it, and it just caused me to be angrier.

I went from disliking people to hating people. I never smiled, and I would snap on anyone that asked me why I didn't smile. I already thought that I was ugly, and my smile was one of the things I hated most about myself. I was just one angry ass individual, and no one cared to wonder why? They just decided to talk bad about me and not to deal with me.

19

The Rape: He Took My Virginity

I MET DEANDRE WHEN I WAS EIGHTEEN YEARS OLD. HE messaged me on Facebook, and it felt good to have a guy interested in me. It felt good to actually attract a guy in real life, rather than the chat line or dating sites. We chatted for a couple of months before we actually met, and he chose to meet me late at night.

I didn't think anything of it, but my mother had a bad feeling about me going out that night. Not only did she tell me, but I could see it all in her face, and I didn't listen.

"Nunni, I don't feel good about this situation or this guy. I don't think you should be going out this late, but you're eighteen so I can't stop you," she told me.

I stood at the church down the street from my house nervous as hell. The outside lights in front of the church beamed on me, but I was still nervous. Soon, I saw a tall figure stumbling as he walked up the stairs and over to me. He reeked of liquor.

"Damn, you lookin' good," Deandre said as he stood in front of me.

"Thank you," I responded dryly.

He aggressively grabbed me by my waist, which scared me a little, and I pushed him back.

"Stop."

"Chill out," he said and grabbed me again.

My nervous level had gone up another ten notches and all I wanted to do was run home, but I tried to coach myself in my mind to just relax.

"You stink. What were you drinking?" I asked.

"Remy and Henny but, damn, let me get a kiss and a hug."

I gave him a friendly hug, but he clearly wasn't feeling that. He gripped me up in an aggressive manner while he grabbed my ass with force. He kissed me and, at first, I kissed him back but then he attempted to stick his tongue in my mouth, which made me turn my head and pull away.

"Damn, if that mouth like that, I wonder what this feel like," he said and grabbed my pussy.

"What do you mean?"

Granted, I was eighteen but, when it came to sex, I wasn't aware of certain things. Of course, my mother taught me sex ed when needed, but I never been around any other guy but Ashanti and he was a young boy, so there wasn't much for me to need to know back then.

"Let me see how wet you is?" he said.

"How?"

"I'ma just rub my dick on ya pussy. That's it."

I should've went with my gut instinct, but I went against my better judgement. "Where we gonna do that at? You can't come back to my house."

"Over there." He pointed to the side of the church.

I stood there, while he walked past me and made his way to the side of the church.

"Come on!" he yelled.

I finally followed him and, for some reason, the wind blew, which sent chills all over my body.

"You want me to take my shorts off?"

"Yea. Take them enough where I can get in between ya legs," he explained.

I did what he told me to do and sat down on the cold ground. He kneeled down and roughly pushed me in my chest onto the ground. I tried to get back up, but he pushed me back down.

"Calm down."

"I don't wanna do this anymore. I'm a virgin and I don't want to do this."

"Man, calm down. I'm only gonna rub the head on ya pussy and then we gonna be done."

I didn't say anything in return. I had no choice but to lie there because he had his hand on my chest and, by now, he was between my legs. He had his dick in his hand and he began to rub it in an up and down motion.

"Damn, you real wet," he said.

"Okay, can I get up now?" I asked.

He didn't answer, and that made me extremely terrified but, before I could protest, his next move took me by surprise. He laid down on top of me, putting all his weight on me, and I was barely able to move. The next thing I felt was a sharp pain ripping through my vagina. I wanted to scream but nothing came out. I wanted to fight, but my hands wouldn't move. I was frozen. I was in shock. I was numb. I didn't know what to do. I was completely stunned by what was going on. It was as if I was having an outer body experience. Like I wanted to fight back, but my spirit watched my body lay there, defenseless.

Deandre tried kissing on me, as if I liked what he was doing. He put his face in my neck while he slid his dick in and out of me. The feeling wasn't pleasurable at all.

"Mmmm," he moaned.

I remember tears falling from the corner of my eyes. I remember looking up at the sky wondering why. Why me? Why was I being hurt like this? Was I that dumb? Was I that unhappy with myself? Was I that desperate? Did I deserve this? Yes, I did. That's how I felt. I knew I was unhappy. I knew I was desperate for male attention because I had never had it before. I never had any man to genuinely like me.

I wasn't sure how much time had gone by, but I remember finally gaining some sort of strength or courage and I pushed him in his chest as hard as I could. He didn't budge much, but he got up on his own afterwards.

"That shit was wet and it felt good. You know you liked that." He stood up and pulled his pants up.

I was still lying on the ground when he got up. My body felt so heavy when I sat up. "Why would you do that? You wasn't supposed to do that."

"You wanted me to do that. Be thankful that I did do it. Niggas don't like big girls. Ain't no nigga gonna want a big girl," he said.

His words stung me like a venomous bee. I believed him because I had been witnessing that very thing since I was eleven years old. I finally got up off the ground and put my panties and shorts back on. I pushed passed him, and he grabbed me by the arm.

"Where you goin'?"

"I'm going home."

"You might as well let me walk you, considering we gon' fuck again."

I didn't say anything in response to what he had just said to me. I continued to walk in silence, as he walked right beside me as if he just didn't violate me. I walked ahead of him as we got closer to my house. I didn't bother to say anything else to him as I ran in the house, locked the door, and ran straight to the bathroom. I pulled my panties and my shorts down before sitting on the toilet. I saw blood in my panties, so I grabbed some tissue and wiped, which was full of blood.

I broke down crying as I grabbed my clothes off the floor and flushed the toilet. I went into my bedroom, grabbed my cellphone, and messaged Deandre on Facebook.

Me: *I'm bleeding.*

Deandre: *I know because I popped ya cherry.*

I cried even more because I knew why I was bleeding. He had taken my virginity, the only thing that I was proud of. I was the only person in my family to keep their virginity to the age of eighteen years old. I never had thoughts about how I would lose my virginity once the time came, but I damn sure didn't know I would lose it in such a painful and awful way.

But, he was right, we did fuck again. I already had low-self-esteem but, once my virginity was taken from me, I went downhill. I had nothing left to be proud of. I had dropped out of school, I had no friends, and I was barely liked by my family. The only thing that made me feel like I was somebody was my virginity and that had been taken from me without any remorse. So, I slept with my rapist willingly.

I never said anything about what happened until six months later. I was afraid that no one would believe me. I mean, I was eighteen, so the law would say I knew better. I also didn't say anything because Deandre was in a gang, and I feared what might've happened to me or my family.

I blamed myself for years after my rape, and I had lost any faith or belief that I had in God. I hated him. If I was His child, how could He allow His child to get raped? How could He allow me to get violated? By the house of God, as some would say. All I know was I didn't believe in him anymore and, as the days went by and the years past, I became angrier with life and who I was.

20

Low Self-Esteem

AFTER MY RAPE, I SHUT DOWN FOR AN ENTIRE YEAR. I was barely eating, I was afraid to go outside, and I was afraid to be around men. Although I was internet dating, I knew those men online couldn't hurt me because they weren't near me. I knew that I wasn't pretty enough to attract men on the outside, which was why I stuck to online dating.

Me being raped proved that men didn't like me at all. I was a big girl, and guys didn't like big girls. I had to just take what was given to me and deal with it. I watched my sisters attract guy after guy. I watched men drool over them, and here I was sitting back lonely. I had never had a boyfriend, and I wanted one. I wanted what they had. I wanted to know what it felt like for a guy to like me, but I didn't.

I was desperate for male attention, and I did everything for it.

I sent nude photos of my pussy, ass, and titties, just hoping I would attract one guy and he would stay around. But, I was ridiculed in the end and my pictures were even posted online by one of the guys that I had shared them with. No guy that I had ever dealt with viewed me as pretty, beautiful, cute, or even attractive. My mental wrapped around the negative things that was always said to me, so there was no room for the positive.

21

Putting Action Behind My Words: Turning My Dreams Into Reality

SEPTEMBER 11TH, 2013 AT 3:49AM, I WAS UP LIKE always. I was thinking about life and how I could help my mother. I was so tired of seeing her struggle. I was so tired of us going without food. I was so tired of everyone using her, and I just wanted to be the one to help her and give her the world. I had never had a job before and, to be honest, I didn't want one. Well, I didn't want to do what everyone else was doing. I could always see myself sitting behind a desk, but I couldn't see myself flipping burgers and that was no shade to anyone that started out that way.

So, I reached out to someone who I had been watching on Facebook for a while. At first, by the name, I thought they were a female, but I soon realized it was a male. Either way, I reached out and I prayed for a response.

Me: *Hello, Mr. Spider. I've been friends with you for some time now, and I look forward to your status updates. They're so inspiring and motivating. I love reading and writing, but I have gotten discouraged because I always felt like I wasn't getting anywhere. I'm only nineteen and I've been writing since I was nine. My dream is to be an author. Is there any advice you could give me? Like this isn't only a dream, but I'm also doing is for my mother. I'm tired of seeing her struggle. I just can't seem to keep the motivation.*

I was sincere when I reached out to Spider. I had saw my mother break down for the last time and I just couldn't take it anymore.

Spider: *Good morning. How are you? If you're willing to follow my lead, I'll teach you how to eat for a lifetime and keep your motivation up. I grew up poor, that's all the motivation you need. If you know what it means to go without. If you're writing and* *want to chase a dream, send me three chapters.*

When Spider wrote me back, I was ecstatic. I sent him the first three chapters of Silver Platter Hoe. He immediately sent me a contract, and I jumped for joy because I was finally getting a chance. No, I didn't do any research; no, I didn't know what it took to be an author; no, I didn't know that I was signing to a snake; and, no, I didn't know that I was about to go through hell and back.

Spider turned out to be a snake but, because he gave me a chance, that's all I looked at. I've learned in life that sometimes all somebody have to do is give someone a chance because sometimes, that's all it takes.

22

Not Knowing My Worth

I MET ANDRE WHEN I WAS EIGHTEEN, BOARDER-LINE nineteen because my birthday was coming soon. I met him six years ago on Instagram in the year of 2014. I thought he was the perfect guy, and what attracted me to him the most was the fact that he took care of his kids. Every time I looked at his Instagram page, he was posting a picture of him and his kids or just his kids. I was attracted to the fact that he was a black man that handled his business.

We had never met, but we always talked on Kik, on the phone, Tagged, or Instagram. When I was raped, I shut down from men, so I had stopped talking to him and he stopped talking to me for whatever reason as well. So, as time went on, I would seek other men.

By now, I was nineteen years old. Quan, whom I had met on Tagged, was a street nigga. He was in a gang, blood to be exact, and he was thirty years old with a daughter. We ended up meeting at a motel called the Econo Lodge, and he was the first guy I had sex with after my rape. I didn't like him physically, but he seemed nice. That was, until he took all of the money I had out of my purse and said he would pay me back, which never happened. That was the last time I talked to him.

"You ugly. You walking around with earrings that say bad and ain't shit bad about you. That's why I fucked you and left. A fly ass nigga like me couldn't be seen walking around with someone like you."

His words cut me like a razor blade with lemon juice on it. I was who he said I was which, was an unattractive female that deserved to be used. He told me that I deserved to get raped, and I believed it. I deserved everything that had happened to me. I had brought on everything that had happened to me. I didn't deserve to be happy. I didn't deserve to be loved. I didn't deserve to live, and Quan made sure he let me know that.

23

Literary Industry

WHEN I FIRST CAME INTO THE INDUSTRY BEING SIGNED to Praise & Glory Publications, I was cautious. Not because of anything I heard, but I just wasn't a people person. I remember me and my family had no electric, and my publisher Spider told me to reach out to a woman named Carla. He said that she would be able to direct me to someone who could help. That's exactly what I needed at the time, so I reached out.

I didn't have shit. I came into the industry with nothing, but I did what I had to do. My mother was ill, and it was my duty to make sure me and my family were good. Even with no electric, I still found a way to get my books done. Couldn't no one tell me I wasn't a go getta!

Me: Hello, our publisher Spider told me to reach out to you. He said that you could direct me to someone who could help with an electric bill?

Carla: Yea, where do you live?

Me: Jersey.

Carla: Have you reached out to anyone? Because in every state there are programs that help you with utility bills.

Me: Yes, both me and my mother have done that, but no one will help because the utility bill is more than one thousand dollars.

Carla: More than one thousand dollars? That's ridiculous. No one should let a bill get that high.

After that conversation, I went back to my publisher and told him how ignorant the lady Carla was to me. He didn't believe me. He went on and on saying how Carla had been loyal and she'd been helping a lot of people on the team. I chucked it up and left it alone. After a while, I noticed how Carla would always make indirect posts about a certain author on the team she didn't like. I knew she was talking about me, but I never said anything.

She even went as far as deleting me off Facebook and then adding me back. I declined her. Now, back then, Facebook had a thing where if someone sent you a friend request and you didn't know them, you could click *I don't know this person*. That must have pissed her off because she posted in the group about a certain author declining her friend request and reporting her, which was completely false.

All of the authors and some readers were commenting saying how whoever it was, was a bitch, they were corny, and so on. Aniya was one of the ones that commented and, considering Spider told me I should look up to her, I felt the need to go in her inbox and tell her that Carla was talking about me. She apologized for commenting without knowing the full situations. I told her it was okay, and we went into having a full-blown conversation.

I thought we hit it off good. I had no idea that Spider was playing us against each other. Because soon after that, I was getting phone calls from Spider telling me how Aniya was telling him how she's better than me and how the books I write were trash.

I was pissed. I'm like, damn, I thought we was supposed to be friends.

"The only way you can get back at her is by dropping books back to back. She can write fast, but you can write fast too. Honestly speaking, she don't write better than you. She just put out a lot of books. I know this, I'm yawl publisher," Spider said during one of our many phone calls.

That's exactly what I did. I wrote book after book. I was hungry, and I refused to let any bitch think she was better than me. That was how I viewed things at the time because Spider was telling me how bad Aniya was talking about it. The sad part about everything was, he was going back telling Aniya and another author, Teri, the same thing.

I remember seeing Aniya make a Facebook post saying how her family will pull up on anybody. I was reading the comments and one of her female cousins posted a picture of her gun saying she comes correct. I was too through at this point because I'm like, these bitches really ready to take it there over some shit I never said?

If anything, the anger should have been directed towards Spider because he was the one saying how

Aniya didn't have any teeth and she was too broke to buy some dentures. Spider was also the same one that told me how dirty Aniya's kids were when he went to New York to visit her. So, Aniya and her family were coming at the wrong one crazy, but my mother, sisters, brother, and father were ready. We never did too much talking, especially when it came to Facebook. We knew what we were about, so it was no need to put on a show for Facebook and that's just how I personally felt.

24

Spider

IT WAS HARD BEING SIGNED TO PRAISE & GLORY Publications. I had to write until my fingers cramped up, and it became very overwhelming at times. I had wrapped up another book, which was Silver Platter Hoe part two, and I received an email that night from Spider telling me that the story was too romantic and that it turned out to be boring. I was pissed. Who the fuck was he to tell me my story was boring? I had bust my ass on that book, so I caught offense that he would say something like that, especially since I didn't feel the need for every book that I wanted to put out to be ratchet.

Spider: *Red, I took you under my wing, I wanted to mentor you, but you can't be so sensitive when someone criticize your work, if you can't handle it, I'll never tell you what*

need to be fix. I take time out of my day to do so because I care and concern. Next, my wife does love the story but she keep it real by telling you it has gotten boring and, like she told you, she's a fan of your work so she would know how other fans think. If a person can even say four chapters of your book is boring, that's bad on the author's name. We did that to save your career; hearing it from us is way better than hearing it from readers, who leave reviews. But trust! You will never have to worry about that again. As far as the last-minute things go's, I'd rather put your book on hold then just let you put out anything. My editors do this to me all the time. I have a book coming out now and, today, they said hey your ending suck, add to it. I don't feel a certain way because they told me that. I get to work and fix it; I know it's for the best. You're not the only author I said hey fix this and that; there is four of them right now and none of them felt a certain way about it because they know I had their *best intentions in heart. If someone truly trying to help you, you can't get sensitive about it; you going to have to grow tough skin to stay in this business. The readers and people speak their mind. Next, we can't force anyone to change their profile picture; if they do it, it's out of love & loyalty; the readers don't have to do nothing, even if they're in the group. You should be proud if only one person you never met changed their profile picture to your book cover and support you. I am. I don't count how many do it, if they do it. I only pay attention to the love, the positive, not the negative. If an author don't do it, then we don't do it for them; we support who support us and love who love us*

Me: *It's not that I can't handle it, it's the fact that I was told at the last minute. Because if I would've known sooner, then I would've been prepared. I was so upset because I was this close to finishing part 3 and then boom, I had to change everything. I'm not sure if that's a good or bad thing. And*

I appreciate you helping me and telling me what I'm doing wrong. I need that because then I'll never learn or grow from my mistakes, so I appreciate all that you're doing for me, but I do feel like my writing isn't good enough from time to time because in all honesty, I'm not feeling part 2. And I know we can't force anyone to change their profile picture, but I see the same people complaining about support, when they be the main ones doing it.

After all that back and forth, I somehow managed to put my feelings to the side and spent the rest of the time writing. December 23rd, 2013 was the day I rewrote Silver Platter Hoe part two in twenty-four hours. I was completely burned out, but that didn't stop Spider from wanting book after book.

25

What Went Up Must Come Down: I Thought It Was Love

THINGS WERE SLOWLY BUT SURELY LOOKING UP FOR ME. I was now a signed author, my books were killing the charts, and I actually had a boyfriend. Andre and I finally met when I was twenty years old. He came to pick me up at my house in his nice ass car, and I was just too geeked. My father wasn't too fond of any guy that I dealt with, but I felt so special that, for once, a guy showed effort in actually liking me. When I left out of the house, he was sitting on the hood of the car waiting for me. He embraced me in the tightest hug ever.

I felt like I was the shit when he let me go and we hopped in his ride. He had some skinny, light skinned male in the backseat who he introduced to me as G. He said it was his brother and I didn't ask anything further questions. I sat back, relaxed, and enjoyed the ride. We made it to Vineland, which was another city in South Jersey, and pretty much where all of the hotels and restaurants were.

I remember it took us some time to find a hotel that would allow us to check in because it was early, like around 11am or so. While we waited, he told me he was hungry, and he wanted to stop to get something to eat, so. we went to Burger King. Andre was all over me.

When it was finally time for us to go to the hotel, I was the one who checked in for us. By the time he got to the room, I was already in my pajamas that I bought for the occasion. Andre didn't waste any time pushing me on the bed, ripping my clothes off, and eating me out.

"Andre, we gotta use condoms," I panted.

"I'm clean. Don't worry," he told me.

He continued to hush me with kisses, until he finally pushed himself inside of me. It hurt like hell because I wasn't sexually active like that. I barely had sex, and I think he could tell because he wasn't gentle with me.

"When's the last time you got checked?" I asked.

"Six months ago," he said.

I believed him, and I didn't question him any further. I was just happy to be around a man that was finally attracted to me. We spent the rest of the night cuddling and talking until we fell asleep.

My mother came to pick us up the next day, and we went to my play sister, Jessica's, house. I was telling her how our night went, and his brother G was sitting there looking dry because he wanted to talk to Jessica, but she wasn't having it.

At this time, I was looking through my bag, and I realized we didn't use the condoms I had bought.

"Here, you can have these. We don't use condoms," I said.

Andre nudged me with his knee. I didn't think anything of it at the time, but I should have. I should have peeped game when I saw it or maybe I wouldn't have gone through what he was about to take me through.

26

What Went Up Must Come Down: I Thought It Was Love

THE NEXT TIME I SAW ANDRE, WE HUNG OUT AT MY PLAY sister, Jessica's, house. He was with his brother G when he came to pick us up from my mother's house. The night started off rocky because he wanted me to buy him some weed, and I just didn't have the money to do it so, instead of telling him that, I told him we couldn't get in contact with the weed man. He was upset, and he cussed me out so bad before we got out of the car. Of course, I didn't say shit back. I mean, what could I say? He had grown to be so verbally abusive towards me in such little time I just dealt with it.

That night, me and Andre had sex all night long and, afterwards, we cuddled. The next morning, I decided to ask him a few things that were bothering me and, before assuming, I decided to try to get the truth.

"Who is Gashon?" I asked.

I could see Andre's lip twitch, and his face flustered with red. He sat up on the bed and gave me a serious look. I could tell that he wanted to either curse me out or slap me in my face for asking him who she was.

"It's my baby mom. Why you going through my Facebook?" he asked.

Now, I never said how or where I knew the lady from, so for him to assume it was from Facebook showed signs of red flags, but I didn't take action like I should have.

"How you know I was on your Facebook?"

"Because I know you was. She commented on my profile picture. Stay off my Facebook Annemarie."

The way he responded felt like a threat, like stay off his Facebook or else sort of thing. I didn't know things were going to go left the way they did because he stormed out of the room. When he came back in, I tried to talk to him, but he pushed me hard.

"Get the fuck away from me, yo."

The push was violent, but the way he spoke to me was so calm. I left out of the room and went into my sister's room. His brother G was sitting on the bed, and I broke down crying. Both him and my sister were confused.

"What happened?" Jessica asked.

"He pushed me because I asked who Gashon was. Like fareal? All I wanted to know was who she was."

I noticed how scared G got. His facial expression turned into a nervous one. That's when I started to question him. I could tell he really didn't want to say much, but he gave me just enough to make a decision I never made. His exact words were: *play him how he playing you.* I didn't think that strong on it, but I should have, considering at the time this was his brother telling me those words.

27

What Went Up Must Come Down: I Thought It Was Love

THE LAST TIME I SAW ANDRE WAS IN OCTOBER. I decided to rent a room, decorate it, and put on something sexy, just so we could have a good time. I had spent almost six hundred dollars in total on everything. I had been texting Andre since 11am that morning, telling him what time to come down.

He didn't come down until 7pm that night and, when he did, he was smelling like straight ass. I had never smelled him before and I was disgusted.

"What is that smell?" I asked.

"I've been working all day," he told me.

I knew he was lying because work wasn't supposed to leave you smelling like ass and stank ass at that. I had a whole attitude. I didn't even want to spend time with him anymore. I guess he realized it, which was why he started eating me out. I didn't enjoy it because I was burning down there for some reason.

"Stop, that don't feel right," I told him.

Andre didn't mind. He still wanted to fuck, and I allowed him to.

The sex was nasty, and it made me feel dirty. I sucked his dick and gagged, but he didn't want me to pull away. He wanted me to throw up on it. I felt belittled, but I didn't want to make him upset so, I did it. He gagged me with his dick, intentionally making me throw up. It was everywhere, and the smell was horrific. After a while, he told me to get up and get on the bed. He laid back and pulled out his phone before grabbing my head and forcing it down to finish sucking his dick. It didn't last but for a good three minutes or so, before he stopped recording and flipped me over on the bed.

He pulled my legs apart and slid inside me. It didn't feel good, nor was it satisfying. I was still burning for whatever reason and the sex was rough. Andre was doing be so hard that my stomach hurt. I was grabbing on to the sheets and anything else I could because I wanted him to stop. When he did, I was happy, but all he wanted me to do was turn around. It was the same way when I turned around and got in doggy style position. He banged me out from the back. At this point, I just closed my eyes and prayed for him to be done. But every time I thought he was finished, he wasn't.

I jumped when I felt him pushing his dick in my ass. I begged for him not to, but he smacked me and told me to shut up before it gets worse. I put my face in the pillow and cried as he fucked me in my ass. It hurt and burned for some reason. The weird part about everything was he didn't do me from the back for a long time. It was as if he just wanted to violate me for some sort of pleasure. Once he was finished, I was disgusted with how bloody the sheets were, and there was even shit on the sheets. He laid down right on it with no problem and pulled out his phone.

"You got some headphones?" he asked.

"No, for what?" I was still trying to get myself together, but I was in pain and I was tired, so I was lying at the end of the bed.

"I wanna call my son."

"What do you need headphones for? I'll just leave out of the room if it's that serious."

"Fuck you, yo! I can't fucking stand you."

I wasn't sure where any of the outbursts came from, so I left and went into the living room of the hotel. I attempted to lie down and sleep on the couch but, when the stench of where he was sitting hit my nose, I got my ass up. I couldn't understand how a grown ass man could be smelling like that but, considering he said he had worked all day, I let the shit slide.

I went back into the bedroom and got in the bed. He turned over and so did I, and I fell asleep. The next morning, I woke up and he was already dressed. I knew we had an extra day because I was the one who paid, so I couldn't understand why he was dressed.

"Where are you going?"

"My grandmother's birthday is today. I gotta go back home for her party," he responded.

Now, I was fully aware of his bullshit and lies. I didn't give a fuck about his grandmother or if there was even a grandmother. I had spent too much money for him to just enjoy himself yesterday and then leave the next day.

"You a damn lie. Ain't no way you leaving ya girl to go to ya grandmother's party and, if that's the case, then why didn't you say that yesterday?" I asked.

"Yo, you really getting on my nerves. I'm leaving now, fuck that," he said.

As he walked by me, he pushed me, which caused me to grab his hoodie because I was done talking to him. He turned around, grabbed me by my neck, and slammed me up against the wall of the hotel room. I remember me punching him in his chest and him constantly slamming me against the wall, yelling at me and telling me not to play with him. By this time, my head was hurting, and I put my hands up in front of my face as a defense.

He stopped and let go of my neck. I assumed he had got a call from his brother because he gathered up everything I bought him and then looked at me.

"I'll come back later alright?"

I nodded my head to him and tried to get myself together before walking him out. His brother G was sitting in the driver's seat and, while Andre put his stuff in the back seat and checked the trunk for something, I hopped in the passenger seat. I told him how nice the truck was, and I asked him when he was going to let me drive it, which in his response he said soon.

That night, Andre never came back. I broke down in tears because I felt so stupid to believe him. I called my mother, telling her how he left and never came back when he was supposed to, and she was pissed. She called him and cussed his ass out and he pleaded the fifth. He gave her all sorts of excuses and then had the nerve to text me and ask me why did I lie? I found myself drinking a bottle of Arbor Mist and Pepsi before crying myself to sleep.

28

He Broke Me: But I Lived

MY MOTHER CAME TO GET ME THE NEXT DAY FROM THE hotel but, before she did, I tried to clean up a little because the room was a mess. There was blood all over the sheets and blanket, throw up on the floor, and Andre had left trash everything. I was so embarrassed for whomever was going to clean the room because it was truly a massacre. I remember placing the last bloody towel in the bathroom and leaving out.

My mother could tell I had been crying because my eyes were puffy. She asked me was I okay, but I didn't want to talk; I just wasn't in the mood. When we got home, the burning sensation got worse. I told my mother and she told me that I probably had a bad yeast infection. I didn't say anything to her, but I knew that, deep down, there was something else wrong.

For three whole days, I was in and out of the emergency room and, each time, they told me nothing was wrong. I knew I wasn't going crazy. I knew that something was wrong because my pussy was on fire and I had never experienced a feeling like I was feeling at the time before. I went back home, and I remember waking up with a high fever the next day. My body was so hot, I had chills, and I could barely get out of bed.

I had to pee, so I took the little bit of strength I did have to get up and go to the bathroom. I winced in pain when I sat on the toilet, and I thought I was going to die when the pee finally came out. I couldn't take it anymore, so I went back into my room and laid on the bed.

"Jessica! Please come here!" I yelled.

"What's wrong?" she asked.

"I need you to look down there and tell me what you see."

I didn't feel comfortable with any woman looking at me but, at that moment, I didn't care. When I opened my legs, the smell was so bad. Jessica had to cover her nose, and I didn't blame her one bit because I was funky.

"It's red Nunni, and it looks inflamed."

She was nervous, so she ran out of the room and called my mother, as well as 911. I got off the bed and opened my legs as much as I could in front of the floor-length mirror I had in my room. I almost passed out at the sight of my vagina. I had green caked up stuff oozing out of my vagina, and my clit on down was fire red.

They took a urine sample and the doctor came back in after about an hour, letting me know that I had Chlamydia, Gonorrhea, a pelvic inflammatory infection, a yeast infection, and a urinary tract infection. One doctor even said I had herpes but, come to find out, my bloodwork got mixed up with another woman who had the same name as me, so I came out in the clear, and my family doctor confirmed that I had nothing to worry about because everything I had was curable.

"Be thankful that you came in when you did. You could have died if you didn't. That's how bad this is," he explained.

I wanted to die right there, even though I could have died. I didn't just feel this way because of the pain I was in, but because I chose to deal with a guy that put my life in danger. My mother didn't want me to talk to him again, but I was persistent. I wanted him to know what he had done.

After playing tug of war with my phone with my mom, she finally let go. She told me to do what I wanted because she didn't care anymore. I called Andre and let him know what I had, and there was a long silence on the phone before he told me he needed to call me back. I was pissed because not only did he not show up, but now he was telling me he had to call me back? I couldn't even get a word in edgewise because he had hung up on me.

When me and Andre spoke again, he revealed that he cheated on me and had unprotected sex with another woman who wasn't so clean. Because of his negligence and mines, I was on several different medications, and I couldn't bathe for at least another week so the smell that came off me was horrific.

Andre kept in touch with me through text. He kept apologizing and saying how he wanted to end his life because of what he took me through. He told me how he went over the girl's house and beat her up, as well as her boyfriend and brother. Although he cheated on me, I actually felt bad because it seemed sincere. I thought he really cared. He even went as far as to calling me, and we had a quick conversation before he had to work.

"Do I still get to hit it or is that done?" Andre asked.

I was so stuck on stupid because I genuinely thought that he didn't know he had any of the STD's that were passed off to me.

"Are you serious? Nigga, sex is the last thing on my mind. You gotta wait until I heal and, when I do, we have to use condoms because this shit ain't no joke," I told him.

After that, I rarely heard from him. He kept telling me how busy he was with work, and how we would see each other again. However, no matter how hard I tried to believe him, I just couldn't. I would go on Facebook and see the same lady named Gashon posting pictures of him or her and him together. She would even tag him in post.

I wasn't confused anymore. I knew that there was something going on, more than what he told me and, whenever I knew the truth about something, I would get the bubble guts. So, when that happened, I knew that I had to get to the bottom of things. I didn't do it right away.

I had been going through so much. I didn't know how much I could take, and Spider continuously hit me up for books, when that was the least of my worries. I was ready to snap on his ass, but my mother told me that, instead of lashing out, I should tell Spider what was going on so that he could understand me, so that's what I did. November 18th, 2014 at 9:13pm, I wrote Spider on Facebook and broke down.

Me: *I'm ready to talk now. I feel like I should be honest with you because I see you like a dad. And if anything ever happens, you will know the truth. I suffer from depression. I'm a cutter, as you can see. I'm not miss perfect. I have a lot going on, and it's gotten truly overwhelming. I keep fighting because I'm tired of quitting. I feel so unloved.*

Yes, my mother loves me but, just in general, I feel so unloved. It has a lot to do with my past and also a lot that has happened to me recently. I was molested when I was younger, and I was raped at eighteen. I've always been depressed. I broke down yesterday and finally told my mother everything, and she was so hurt that her blood pressure went up and she had to be rushed to the hospital.

I put on a smile everyday covering up everything I'm going through. The guy that I'd been dealing with did everything in his power to hurt me. He broke the little bit of heart that I had left. One of the girls he messed with is cool with a lot of people in the book industry. He gave me numerous std's and, even after all of that, I still loved him. I feel like a failure because right now, me and my family have no food and no heat.

I'm writing my ass off fighting for respect from the readers because I know I have talent. No one has ever given me a chance; that's why I take when people criticize my writing so hard. I've been trying to save money and it's just not working because the bills just keep coming. My mother is a strong woman and she does everything in her power to stay strong and do everything she can to make sure we're okay.

She doesn't ask me for money and she hates when I help out, but I live here too and it wouldn't be right if I didn't. My mother looks so stressed and you can tell that she's tired. She's in therapy now, so she's never home but she comes and visit us every day. I'm fighting to stay strong; all I've been doing is praying. The guy I was dealing with just stopped.

I never knew we were done, he just stopped coming to see me and stopped calling and texting. When I was rushed to the hospital, they said I could've died. I told him, and he never came. The only one that was there was my mother. I know there's people out there who has and is going through worse, but this is my truth and, no, I'm not crazy; this is just how I handle my situations.

I remember that day like it was yesterday, and I still got the cuts on my arms to prove it. That year was so hard for me, and through the months of September through December was very trying for me. I thought opening up to Spider would make things better because at the time, I did see him as a second dad. He seemed so caring and understanding, but my gut always told me that something wasn't right about him.

Spider: *This was very deep. I'll call you soon.*

When he called me, he spoke nothing but bullshit. Instead of him giving me kind words or helping, the only thing he said was that I needed to keep writing more books regardless of what I went through. He couldn't understand how I never had food and how we were never able to keep up with the bills. I didn't like to feel judged or to be judged. I didn't appreciate when someone spoke down on me about my struggles. The way he came off was one of the very reasons why I kept everything so bottled in.

I had a gut feeling that shit wasn't right. That was one thing that my mother always told me, "Always go with your gut." No matter how much the truth was there, I ignored it. I guess once he realized that I was catching on to the snake shit, he hit me with a sales report that showed me that I had made a few grand. The shit worked too. Me and my family had been struggling for years. However, my mother always made a way.

But, I was tired of that. I was tired of her making a way. I had never seen more than three hundred dollars before so, when I saw that I was making a couple thousands, I was hyped. I looked at it like I could finally take care of my family. But, I realized in the end, I was too eager. I allowed the thought of never struggling again overpower what was in front of my face the entire time. But, it wasn't just me. This nigga preyed on those who didn't have, those who were in need, or those he knew he could easily manipulate.

29

Karma Came Back Ten-Fold

I REALIZED JUST HOW HEARTLESS SPIDER WAS WHEN one of his former authors died. I was so crushed because she died due to her not being able to get her medicine because he'd stopped paying her. I remember the last time her and I spoke, we got into an argument over Spider.

Me: *CiCi called you a ratchet ass nigga, and I asked her was she mad about her eighty-six dollars and, if so, I could send it to her.*

Spider: *LOL.*

Here I was trying to be smart and throw shade about CiCi's pay, not knowing that he wasn't paying her at all. She was ill, and she couldn't even afford her meds because the money she earned was taken from her. I was crushed when I saw on Facebook that they found her dead. I laughed at her about making eighty-six dollars, and I had no clue that I would soon be in her same shoes.

Soon after that, I started to notice that me and Spider would get into it over every little thing. He was trying to control me, and I just wasn't for it. I was starting to see him for who he was, and that was a major turn off. He was trying to control me every step of the way and, no matter how much I tried to compromise with him, things got worse.

Spider: *Anne, I have gotten to the point with you where I am completely turned off. You are ungrateful and can't be mentored. Your attitude lately has been very disrespectful, and I do and have done a lot for you. Every time me or my wife gives you a suggestion about anything or guide you the right way, we get a problem and an attitude.*

I've done nothing but try and push and guide you, and you give me attitude. The free books, prices, cover ideas, everything is to build your name as an author and you don't appreciate it. I've sent you a computer to help better your career and because I try to mentor you, I get "this is aggravating, I don't want to do it." Fine, I no longer care. Whatever cover you want, whatever price you want, the pages of your books, and all the extra you want to do with them, do it.

I could have easily been like any other publisher and not give a damn and let you do those things, not try to help better you, etc., but I wasn't but now I will be. And this is what we will do. Once I receive my ten books from Praise & Glory Publications, you can leave. Sign with another company or give up all together, doesn't make a difference to me. What hurts is I put my all into you, and I get your nasty ass attitude handed back to me.

Me: *This has nothing to do with my attitude. I bit my tongue about a lot. No matter what I've seen or heard, I said fuck them; I'm riding with you. But, what I dislike is that if I feel like I'm unhappy, you just tell me what I want to hear and that's something I dislike. This has nothing to do with what you and ya wife do, but what's the problem* *with letting me know that changes are gonna be made? We bump heads and that's the problem*

Spider: *You think what I'm doing for you is to hurt you? Your career is rising, your checks are getting bigger, everything is happening for you and you get upset because I told you not to put a part 5 sneak peek of a different series behind your book? You would have been better off doing a sneak peek for part one! We bump heads because of your attitude and not being coachable*

Me: *How am I not coachable? I listen to what you say, but I also have my own mind. I put a sneak peek of Byron in the back of sph3, so what was the difference between this one and that one? & maybe you see something I don't because I still feel unsuccessful. I don't like a lot of stuff and I'im not like everyone else who can just sweep stuff under the rug*

Spider: *You are because whenever I give you a suggestion, you get mad and discouraged. No one said you don't have your own mind but, if I see something that will better you, I will speak on it. The difference with Byron is that IT WAS A SNEEK PEAK OF PART 1. If no one has read Byron, they are getting a piece of the beginning. You tried to put a sneak peek of an end of a series. You really though that made sense?*

So, if someone is reading Honey Dipp and never read Silver Platter Hoe, they gone get a SNEAK peak of the end of the series? That what I'm saying. This is what you are mad at. You feel unsuccessful, but you your books are selling, you're on the bestsellers, people know who you are, you are now making four figures, not even adding what your full priced books will make are you serious?

Your problem is that you are ungrateful and it's nothing else to it. You have nothing to be mad or complain about but, still, you find some pettiness about a sneak peek, worried about what everyone else is doing, quick to scream favoritism, when you were one of my favorites! You drop two books a month, all my authors don't do that. I haven't been even dropping my own, but you don't trust no one, you're uncomfortable? Sure.

Me: *I have read books from top authors that did what I did. The way I was looking at it is that if Honey Dipp is the first book someone reads of mines and they see Silver Platter Hoe 5, its going to make them search the series and read it for themselves. I didn't look at it the way you did. And there's nothing ungrateful about ne because I appreciate everything people do for me, but I also don't wana feel like I'm just being told what I wanna hear and that's how I felt SOMETIMES.*

It just wasn't about the sneak peek. I understand you been in the game longer than me, and I understand you be tryna help me; I'm not blind to that. We bumped heads over my sph4 cover; the cover I wanted was the one I wanted, but you wanted me to go with the cover you wanted. The way you made me feel was like my books wasn't going to make any sales because of the cover. & yes, I have bad trust issues with men and that's why I always say what's on my mind, because of that.

How I felt was how I felt. Spider made me feel like if it wasn't his way, then my books weren't going to sell. He made me feel like he made me when, in all reality, he didn't make me. He gave me exposure, but it was me busting my ass writing the books. But, regardless of how much me and Spider argued, I noticed he would do things to make me forget about what took place days before.

Me: Hey, Mr. Spider. I am still seeing that Closed Legs Don't Get Fed has a lot of errors. I'm getting more 1 stars than five stars, and I understand that not everyone will like my work, but it seems like Dope Dick and Closed Legs Don't Get Fed is just receiving bad reviews. Like it's really hard for me to have worked so hard on a book and they receive so many one-star reviews.

Regardless, if the readers felt like I just put out shit, I knew that I cared about my work. I would always contact Spider about my edits and what the readers were saying, and he would always tell me not to worry about it. Only, this particular day when I confronted him about the edits, instead of a reply, he sent me my sales reports.

Me: Omg! Mr. Spider, I just burst into tears. I made 11,619 and I'll be getting 5,809. God is so good, I ain't been an author a year yet and ma money is just going on. Idk what to say. I'm so thankful. I went from making 150 to 5k

I was hype as hell. I had never made or witnessed that much money in my life. I felt like I was on top of the world. I couldn't wait to go food shopping and fill up our fridge. I couldn't wait to help my mother pay back bills that were due. It was going to feel so good to do for my family.

Spider: Lol told you, to trust me. Keep going and it will be more

Me: Smh them haters ain't stop nothing

Spider: I told you, more contests, we need to take over that list, and you need to do a part 4 lol. haters didn't stop shit. One book alone made 3k; can you picture if we get all your new books on that list?

Me: That would be awesome. I need part 2 to make that much. I'll hit them with a Dope Dick part 2, Byron 2, Twisted Faith next month. December, I'll hit then with part 3 of Closed Legs Don't Get Fed, Trina spin off, Desire and Rell, and then for the new year sph 6!

I was a total jackass to let those dollar signs block my vision from what was really going on. Spider was doing what he did best, milking me like the cow I was. He preyed on people who needed help and, once he got you under his wing, it was over from there. Spider even went as far as to promising to buy me a truck. I remember hitting him up about it because times were getting rough around my way once again.

Me: Hey Mr. Spider. I did two email blasts. Anywho, they just took our truck. We didn't have the money to keep it. Are you sure I will be getting my car next month?

Spider: Yes, for your birthday.

Around this time, my mother's truck had been repoed because we couldn't keep up with the payments. I know people are like damn, but you just made five grand. The money came in fast, but it left just as quick.

30

The Confession: Finding Out the Truth

ALTHOUGH HE HAD STOPPED TALKING TO ME, I HAD hope that he would reach out to me. So, I gave Andre chance after chance to come clean but, three days before my 21st birthday, I finally had enough when she posted about him for the last time.

Me: **Hey. You don't know me, but I wanted to know if you had a moment to talk? I don't want any problems because I'm pregnant.**

Gashon: **Hey. What's up? Sure. Talk about what?**

Me: **I think we're dealing with the same guy.**

Gashon: **Omg. What's your number?**

I gave her my number and she called me right away. My exact words to her were, "So, wait, are you and Andre really together?"

"Yea, he's downstairs; we just got finished having sex. He's smoking a blunt now," she replied.

I broke down. My stomach was in knots because the truth had just been confirmed. We had an hour conversation, and she revealed that Andre hadn't had a job in ten years. He sold pills, weed, and he even robbed people. She explained that Andre had been living with her for the last three years and that he wanted her to get her tubes untied so that they could have a baby together. I told her how he called her slow and said that he'd been broke it off with her and that the reason she was still posting about him was because she couldn't get over him. She went on to tell her how she tried leaving him plenty of times and how he would beg her not to.

I couldn't believe my ears. I remember crying like I had just lost my best friend. The pain, the hurt, the audacity of his nasty ass. When I told her about me ending up in the hospital, her response made me want to jump through the phone and snatch her tongue out of her mouth.

"I wish I would have known about you because he does this to all the girls he come across. You're not the only one, but I hate that I couldn't have warned you. You're so young."

I was sick to my fucking stomach. As a mother who has a daughter, the nerve of her to be okay with what this man was doing. To women, black women at that.

"How can you deal with that?" I asked.

"As long as he don't bring that drama here, I'm good because he knows where home is," she said.

After I got off the phone with her, I called my mother and broke down so bad. That same night, she called Andre but got no answer. However, he did text her back and said he would reach out to her another time. Now, let's fast forward to three days later, which was my twenty-first birthday. I was in bed knocked out when my sister Dani came in.

"Girl, what is you still doing in bed sleep?" she asked.

I was in no mood. I didn't care about my birthday at all. When I found out that Andre and the girl Gashon were still together, I was crushed because she claimed that she was so done with him and that she was putting him out. She even went as far as to send me a video of all his stuff packed. I was happy because I thought that he was about to get put out.

"He still with her, Dani," I cried.

"Girl, you gotta get over that. She wasn't going to leave him and he wasn't going to leave her because she's a dumb ass bitch. Niggas love dumb bitches. She's giving him money, a place to stay, and he's allowed to cheat in peace. What nigga won't want that?" she told me.

I didn't understand it, none of it, but I cried and cried some more until she finally told me to get my ass up and get dressed. That I did, and we ended up going to Dave and Buster's for my twenty-first birthday. I had fun but ended up paying for everything. My stuff, and my sister's stuff. It didn't bother me at first because I was out having fun and trying to clear my mind.

That night, we ended up going to my sister's boyfriend's house, who was married. I was tired and my allergies had started acting up, so I went straight to sleep. The next morning, I woke up and my sister was walking around the house in a thong. That's it, just a thong, nothing else. When her boyfriend came downstairs, his wife was behind him. I sat back on the couch in complete shock. Like, what the fuck is going on here?

Her boyfriend introduced me to his wife, as if my sister wasn't sitting on the couch in a thong smoking a blunt like it was normal. It was at that moment, I knew I needed to get the hell up out of there.

31

Mental Break Down

Everything seemed to have been triggering me since the Andre situation. My mental state was truly screwed up, and I didn't realize it until, one day, I was heating me up some food in the microwave and my father came out needing to use the microwave as well. Instead of him asking me to let him know when I was done, he took my food out of the microwave and threw it to the side.

"Why couldn't you just wait until I was done using the microwave?" I asked.

"Muthafucker, I'm not waiting for shit. Ya fat ass don't need this food anyway.

It was at that point that something came over me. "I'm so fucking tired of you!" I screamed.

"Hey, what is going on in there!" my mother asked; she was using the bathroom.

"Muthafucker, what ya dumb ass say?"

"I didn't stutter. You always walking around here doing ignorant shit and we can't say nothing. I'm tired of that!"

"I'm tired of you too, you stupid fat bitch!"

"Nunni, come here!" my mother yelled.

I went to the bathroom and all I could see was red. "What? Why are you calling me? You didn't just hear him call me a stupid fat bitch and you calling me?"

I wasn't sure what exactly happened next, but all I knew was that I had a meat cleaver in my hand trying to slice my father up, and my brother took me down like a football player. That night, my mother called the cops on me. I understood that I was the aggressor, but why was it okay for him to talk to me like that? Not only was I his daughter, but I was his baby girl whom was receiving the same treatment from men that he was giving me.

32

Used

IT WAS HARD GETTING OVER ANDRE. A FEW DAYS AFTER my birthday, it was Gashon's birthday and, when she uploaded pictures of them all hugged up, it confirmed everything once again. What made it so bad was the fact that Andre had called my mother. He told her how he was sorry for everything that happened, and that he and Gashon were not together; he was just using her for her money so that he could get himself an apartment out in Atlantic City, New Jersey.

He told my mother to tell me to just be a little patient with him and we would better together. Andre even said that the MK bag he bought her was with her own money that she had given him previously. I wanted to believe everything he said, but the proof was in the pudding. Yet, my ass still had a hint of hope. That was, until we had lost touch completely and he hit me up months later saying he was about to go to jail if he didn't pay his fines.

He asked me for five hundred dollars, and I gave it to him. I gave it to him because I thought that we would get back together. He played the fuck out of me because that was the last time I had heard from him for a while. I would peek in on his Instagram and his ass had bought a new car and was living life. I was so livid. I was so hurt. I was embarrassed, I was hurt, I felt hopeless, and stupid all in one. The next time I heard from Andre was due to me reaching out to him, letting him know how dirty he was. I had found numerous sex videos of him on Pornhub, and I got sick to my stomach because he was fucking each female raw.

That was the night he told me he knew he had an STD and that he gave it to me on purpose. His words were, "You didn't ask, so I didn't tell." I couldn't understand it because the STD's I had were curable but, after speaking to my doctor, she explained the Chlamydia could linger for a long time, which was why she told me that whoever I was dealing with had a high strain of it, and they weren't taking their medicine.

I wanted to get Andre killed. How could someone do something like that? I even thought I was pregnant, but I went through pseudocyesis. I didn't know until more tests were ran that I actually wasn't pregnant. I was hurt because I wanted a baby, I wanted my baby. I was going around with the guilt of me having a miscarriage because the STD's I had and, all along, I was never pregnant.

33

Caught Between A Rock and A Hard Place: The Beginning of the End of My Career

My PERSONAL LIFE WAS COMPLETELY SHATTERED, AND my career was now going downhill. Before I left Praise & Glory Publications, Spider had crowned me The Princess Of Urban Fiction. I thought the name was cute, but I knew it would ruffle some feathers.

"I don't know if putting the princess of urban on my books is a good idea," I told him.

"It's a good idea because I said it is. I sign your checks. So, what I say goes," he stated.

I can't front. I kept my mouth shut about a lot because my money was threatened. Some would probably think I sold my soul. But, the truth is, I was afraid. Afraid to go hungry again. Afraid to be homeless again. Afraid to see my mother struggle again. I found out the hard way that when you give a man the power to feed you, you also give him the power to starve you.

Although I didn't like the way he spoke to me, I kept my mouth shut. But, just like I expected, crowning me The Princess Of Urban Fiction backfired. I was getting hate all over, in book groups and on readers pages. Every time I reached back out to Spider, he would make up some excuse saying they were "haters" and to not worry about what they were saying. I was nothing more than a puppet to Spider. He wanted book after book, and I kept writing. As I look back, I brought a lot of stuff on myself out of fear. If only I had been just a little bit stronger, none of what happened would have happened.

34

Don't Believe the Hype: Even Salt Looks Like Sugar

I REMEMBER SPIDER TELLING ME ABOUT ONE OF HIS former authors. He kicked her back in so bad, and even went to telling me how he paid for her to get an abortion. Without me knowing the full facts and feeling like if I sided with Shyanna I would get my money taken, I decided to side with Spider. He was the one threatening my money and I didn't want to get on his bad side anymore.

Me: *As far as Shyanna, she's handling things unprofessional. How she's getting 80+ likes on these statuses, I have no clue. But people dwell on negativity.*

All along, Shyanna had been keeping it real from jump and, although her delivery was messed up at times, I realized after a while, she meant no harm. I felt fucked up for talking bad about her. I felt bad for not having another black woman's back when she was trying to speak her truth. The shit was wrong on my behalf and that's why karma smacked my ass hard as hell in the face. Karma made sure I felt exactly what Shyanna felt, and it hurt like hell. I knew then to never speak on what I didn't know because there were always more sides to a story.

Spider would always say that I needed to focus on putting out another book. He didn't care that I was being dragged on Facebook and my career was going down the drain. His main focus was me putting more money in his pockets. Spider even went as far as to telling me he would buy me a house, as long as I brought my mother with me. He wanted to sleep with my mother, and he said he didn't mind if I joined in. So, I had to deal with him threatening my money, as well as him trying to sleep with me and my mother, on top of getting bashed about being the Princess Of Urban fiction.

One reader in particular named Neeka, who actually used to be a reader of mine, was pissed about the name. She went into a well-known Essence bestselling author group bashing the hell out of me.

I didn't know about it until another reader sent me a screenshot because I had left this particular author group a long time ago. It was too messy and way too much drama and author bashing going on.

When I saw the screenshot, I deleted Neeka. I didn't appreciate the fake love. One minute you're giving me five-star ratings and, then, the next minute, you're in a group bashing me? Once I deleted her, she decided to make an even bigger scene by updating a status saying the princess of urban deleted her. Her bandwagon ass friends hopped on the post talking about how trash my books were and how they wish they could call Amazon to report me.

These were all female readers who once supported me but, whenever Neeka made a post bashing an author, they were right behind her. It went from just saying my books were trash to talking about my weight. They were passing my picture around and it semi went viral due to the insults.

I was labeled as a punk bitch in the industry because I didn't respond when I was dragged through the mud. I sat and cried for days because I was angry and hurt. I was angry because I couldn't drag a bitch, but I was hurt because everything I had worked for had been snatched away from me in a matter of weeks.

I remember sitting down with my mother and her exact words were, "WE all know you can fight, and WE all know you'll be the first one to pop. Ain't none of those scandalous ass bitches tag you. What did they do? Post your picture and call you fat. None of them had the balls to come to you directly and, for the ones who attempted, what did they do? They blocked you right after they sent the message. Stop stepping off your throne for people that ain't worth your time. Yea, your career may be a little shaky right now, but I promise you it's going to bounce back. You know mommy don't condone violence but, if any one of those females that threatened to pull up about that, tell them to come on."

35

Friend or Foes: The Butt of the Joke

I WAS STILL SIGNED TO PRAISE & GLORY PUBLICATIONS through contract but, in my mind, I had already left. I was handling things accordingly because Spider still had control over my money, and things were bad where I lived.

Shyanna, DeeDee, Terry, and Shamiya all had added me to a group chat that was about Spider. We were all discussing the things that had been said and done to us, and we were all thinking of ways to take him down because we were just tired of him and his shit. I was the only one still signed to him and, once I made that clear, they all went to bashing me behind my back. I didn't know this until Shyanna got tired of them talking about me and she came to me.

"Look Reds, they all talking about you and I just got tired of it. I said, instead of talking about that girl, go head and tell her how yawl feel. Since, they won't do it, I will. You need to just take ya books down and self-publish," Shyanna told me.

I didn't respect any of them for talking about me, but I respected the fact that Shyanna got tired and finally decided to come to me as a woman about how she felt. Everyone wanted me to do what they wanted me to do, but how many of them were going to pay my bills once Spider took my money? Because that's exactly what he did. He snatched everything from me once I left him so, by this time, I went back into a depressed state. Because I had given Andre my last and Spider had stopped paying me because I left his company. A whole twenty-two-thousand-dollar check snatched from me because he said *I didn't deserve it*.

In the midst of all this, a female publisher that I'm going to refer to as Michelle tried signing me, but she was the same female publisher that was going back and forth to Spider telling him how dumb I was for signing a fifteen-book contract.

She said that if he could get me, then why couldn't she? I never signed a contract with her because she just came off as fraud to me. She would send me pictures of houses and cars, but they were straight off google. She even said how she had ghost written the book *Dutch* and how another well-known author did her dirty after she had ghostwritten most of her books.

That was just something I couldn't believe, and I didn't. Once I let her know that I wasn't interested in signing, she said too late; she'd already getting covers made. That's when I knew this lady was batshit crazy. I stopped responding to her Facebook messages and, then, she started commenting her my post. When I ignored her, she deleted me and updated a status about me, which Aniya called me and told me about. That's when I went off. I was so fed up with people coming at me, when I didn't do shit to begin with. I posted all of our messages and told the lady how crazy she was.

Michelle inboxed me and said she would take a flight, so we could fight. It was over from that point on because my sister Linette was on her ass and so was my mother, Maria. My father even intervened.

"If she wants to come all the way to Jersey to get her ass beat, tell her ass to come on!"

Once my family got on her ass, she blocked them and updated another status about me, only this time it was a picture of me with a caption that said: *one word, diet.*

Aniya called me and screenshot the post of her and some other females calling me fat, saying I needed a waist trainer, and more. Of course, I was hurt, but I was tired of fighting. I had no more fight in me. Shit went from bad to worse and, out of all people, I thought Aniya should have had my back, but she didn't. She was front and center to tell me about when I was being talked about, but not once did she ever defend me, and not that it was her obligation to do so because she had a brand to protect as well but, if you're going to screenshot stuff to me and if you tell me how wrong it is in my inbox, why not tell them they were wrong? It's not about arguing, nor is it about fighting. It was about backing up your actions. This was the same woman that called me 'sis'.

36

Trying to Rebuild: Game Plan

IT WAS NEAR THE END OF 2015 AND I WASN'T MAKING any money. I was still being talked about on Facebook, and I was still trying to find a way out. I had talked to Vick, who was another well-known publisher and author. He had his eye on me for a while, but I didn't sign to him because I heard he pimped out a fourteen-year-old girl. I didn't want any parts of anyone who had done something like that, although I didn't know all of the facts. I should have given him a chance when I had a past too but, like I said before, a lot of things I brought on myself. Because even after all he'd heard about me, he still wanted to sign me.

So, once I declined him, his friend Calvin, who was another well-known author and publisher, came to me trying to sign me. He asked for my number and I gave it to him, which he called me in seconds.

"I think we should do a collab together," he said.

"Really? I'm down. I think that would be a good look. But, it has to be a fifty-fifty split down. I'm not accepting pennies because I write some dope ass books," I explained.

"Let me see what I can do, and then I'll give you a call back."

I told him cool, and I allowed him to do that so, when he called back, he had all kinds of excuses. He told me that he couldn't do the fifty-fifty split down and that he couldn't do that collaboration either. But, he did want me to write a book under him called *I like my bitches bbw*. He said he'd been seeing how people were trash talking me and my weight and he wanted me to embrace it.

I was disgusted on how he came off. That wasn't a book title I would have chosen for myself and I didn't like what it represented. I didn't hesitate to decline his offer. Then, I found out he was in prison so that was a definite no go.

I was still sticking to my guns, although I barely had a career. I decided to just go ahead and self-publish my books so that I could at least make a couple of dollars. It worked because I was making just that, a couple of dollars. But, when push came to shove, only one person ended up giving me a chance and that was Tommy. He signed me, even after all the bad he heard about me.

37

Internet Dating

I REMEMBER MEETING A GUY OFF TAGGED. HE SEEMED so nice and different. I didn't remember his name but, if I saw him again, I would surely remember his face.

I didn't want to do it, but I wanted him to like me. The moment he slid his dick inside me, I regretted everything after. He was forceful, rough, and angry. He turned into a completely different person. I tried to push him back but, at that point, it was too late. He slammed his dick in and out of me like I was used goods. It was hard, brutal, and I knew this because of how my pussy burned from being torn. The car was shaking, and I begged for him to stop. I didn't know how long he fucked me for but, when he was finished, he pulled out, took the condom off, and threw it on the floor of the backseat.

He got out of the car, got in the driver's seat, and, all of a sudden, his phone rang.

"Hello? I'll be there." He ended the call and looked back at me. "I gotta go pick my mother up, so I'ma drop you off and come pick you up tonight."

"Okay," I said as I tried to get myself together.

I got back in the passenger seat and put my seatbelt on. I couldn't want to get home and shower. I felt dirty and my panties got wetter and wetter during the drive home. He dropped me off on the corner he picked me up from.

"Call me and let me know when you're ready," he said.

"Okay, I'll see you tonight," I told him before closing his door.

I walked home with a limp and, when I finally got to the house, I went straight to the bathroom. I pulled my panties down and saw that the seat was filled with blood. I grabbed some tissue and wiped, and blood covered it. I didn't know how to feel. All I know was that it gave me déjà vu, like the night I was raped.

Not only that, but that was the last time I heard from him. I called and text him for the remainder of that day, up until he blocked me. It was a couple months later when I found out that I wasn't the only female he had done that to.

Then, there was another time where I had met a guy off Tagged, and we ended up meeting. He drove me all the way to Willingboro, New Jersey to a hotel. We fucked and, afterwards, he told me that he would be right back. After about an hour, I finally tried reaching out to him and got no response. I went down to the lobby to ask the man at the front desk did he know where my friend Sean went.

"Who?" he asked.

I showed him a picture of Sean, and he shook his head no.

"His name isn't Sean, ma'am, but I did see him. He left about an hour ago," he revealed.

"Are you sure?" I asked.

He nodded his head yes. I tried calling and texting the man who I knew as Sean, and I got no response. I was stuck, hours away, and I had no way to get home and no money. He had fucked me and left me in the hotel room with a bottle of water. If it wasn't for Jessica, I would have never gotten home, and the embarrassment in my heart wouldn't allow me to cry about the way I had been played.

38

Saving Jimmy

I KNEW THAT I WAS A GOOD PERSON BUT, WITH SO MUCH bad shit happening to me, I just felt like I was a fucked-up person. Because there was no way that so much fucked-up shit could happen to a good person. I was hurting inside. I had a lot of anger built up inside of me. But, no matter what, whenever someone needed me, I was there. I couldn't understand how I would rather help someone else or see someone else smile, although I was broken up.

I remember lying down in my bed asleep one day when I heard my phone ring. I hated being woken up out of my sleep, and I had all intentions on ignoring the call, but something told me to pick it up.

"Hello?"

I heard gurgling sounds coming from the other end. I looked at my phone and saw that it was my brother that had called me.

"Hello!" I screamed.

"Help me," he gasped.

I was scared shitless. I didn't know what to do, but I jumped my ass out of bed and the first place I ran was down to the basement because his bedroom was down there. I was halfway down the stairs before jumping down the rest, when I saw my brother hanging from a pole from the ceiling. Foam was coming out of his mouth and his veins were bulging on the side of his head and forehead. I tried to lift him up, but he was too heavy. He tried pointing at something and I was panicking while trying to figure out what he's pointing at and, then, finally, I see a stool. I grabbed the stool and put it under him, so he could stand up. I moved at a fast past trying to get the cord from around his neck and, then, once I did, he collapsed into my arms.

"Jimmy, what are you doing! Why would you do this? What's going on? Talk to me!" I cried as I held him.

He pushed me away and crawled into his bedroom. My hands were shaking, and my mouth was as dry as a desert. I couldn't believe that I had just saved my brother from killing himself. I couldn't believe that I had just witnessed something like that. I had never been so scared in my life, and I never wanted to feel like that again.

39

He Loves Me, He Loves Me Not

MONTHS AFTER, I HAD YET ANOTHER BAD EXPERIENCE on Tagged; I met another guy named Dew. He hit me up, and one thing led to another and we were pretty much inseparable. But, he was verbally abusive, and he had given me an STD.

"Fuck you, you dirty bitch. I ain't give you shit. You better ask that nigga that raped you about that shit," he spat.

I had been dealing with Dew for two years, and he took me through hell and back. I tried to settle down with him and even get a place with him. No matter how much he verbally abused me, I still had hope for us. He never took any of my money, and I thought that he was attracted to me because he said he only liked big girls. I believed him until I wanted to try a certain sex position.

"I'm not doing that with ya big ass. Get outta here and leave that shit to the skinny girls. Be lucky I'm even fucking you."

I told my mother what he said, and she was disgusted. She hated how I took so much from guys, and she always tried to tell me how much I deserved better. But, it didn't matter what she said, it was what they said. If every guy I came across treated me the same way, then I must've deserved that treatment, right?

40

Trying To Rebuild: Game Plan

I HAD JUST SIGNED TO ANOTHER PUBLISHER NAMED Rocky and I was going under a pen name, but Dollar Bill, the CEO of Behind The Bars Publications, was seeking for me to sign to him. I just wasn't with it. I had been burned in the industry so much that I didn't want to sign with anyone else. He explained how he had been watching me and wanting me since day one, and how he could get my name Reds Johnson back, and he could get my books in stores. I couldn't front and act like that didn't spark my interest because my dream was to have my books in stores.

I had no clue that Dollar Bill was in prison because if I did, then I wouldn't have given him any sort of conversation. Dollar Bill knew that I wasn't budging, so he had his COO Shawna talk to me. I was already going through hell, and she came to me so innocent, so sweet, and so caring. It was Queen this and Queen that. I ended up venting to her about everything that I had been going through, and all she did was listen. It felt so good for someone to listen to me besides my mother.

She ended up persuading me to sign, and my dumb ass did. The backlash I received was crazy, and I couldn't understand it. So many people were telling me I was going to regret it. I told Dollar Bill and he said they were just bitter people. My gut told me otherwise, but I was already in the contract.

41

More Than A Friend?

ME AND SHAWNA WAS SO COOL THAT SHAWNA HAD hooked me up with one of her ex's friends that lived in Louisiana. He was tall, dark, and finer than a muthafucka. He sent me a picture of his dick the first night we started talking and, before I sent him a nude photo back, I sent it to Shawna for her approval. I was a chunky girl and I wanted to know if the picture was sexy enough. I thought that, since me and Shawna was best friends, I could share stuff like that with her.

Shawna wanted to send the picture to Dollar Bill. Now, considering I had sent her a nude full body shot, I was thinking she was going to do the same thing. When my phone went off, I opened the message and in clear view was Shawna's pussy.

"What the fuck is that?" I asked.

"That's my kitty when I'm horny," she replied.

"And he likes that?"

I ain't never saw no vagina that looked as bad as Shawna's. It looked swollen and infected. Her lips were shriveled up and her clit looked like it was about to disconnect from her body. I was so disgusted. Considering I told my mother everything, this was no different. I had to share it with something and that somebody was her.

"Mom, Shawna sent me a picture of her stuff," I stated.

"Why is she sending you pussy shots?" she asked.

"Well, I guess because I sent her a picture of me that she felt like it was alright to send that."

"Nah, Nunni, I don't like the vibe that bitch gives me. I already been feeling funny about her and her extra nice ass. I want you to fall back off her because she's sneaky and, pretty soon, she'll be asking you to fuck her."

My mother was right because Shawna did ask me would I have a threesome with her and the male friend of hers that she had introduced me to. It was just a lot of weird shit going on at Behind The Bars Publications. Not only did Shawna try to have a threesome with me, but she was in a relationship with Dollar Bill, and he was in a relationship with several of his authors, as well as his readers; Missy, Brook, Morgan, April, and Apryl were all his girlfriends.

"We protect him. He's our Kind. He's our God because the black man is God," Shawna told me.

I should've gotten the fuck away from them when she said that, but I didn't. I sat back, hoping that something better would come so that I wouldn't fall flat on my face the way that I did before Dollar Bill got to me.

42

Lies and Betrayal

I HAD BEEN DEALING WITH RAH FOR ALMOST A YEAR. HE was also signed to Behind The Bars Publications. He was from Philly and had grew up in my neck of the woods. I started out promoting for him as a friend, and he saw the real in me, so he asked me out. I loved him something serious, but I wasn't in love with him. I didn't mind that he was in prison. I was a rider regardless, and I damn near melted every time I received a call from Coal Township Prison.

Things weren't always peaches and cream. I had one female in particular named Larissa that always came at me indirectly, and I knew she was talking about me because she always referred to the girl as a fat bitch that keeps trying to take her man. I dealt with the backlash from her and her best friend Bonni. The shit became stressful after a while and I would always tell Rah that he had no idea what I had to deal with while being with him and supporting him.

"Bae, just don't worry about them. Them bitches just jealous."

He would always tell me the same thing, and I just didn't believe him. I didn't believe him because when I would go to him and he would tell me that he handled the situation, I wondered how the hell did you handle anything if you don't talk to her?

Things didn't go haywire until December 1st, 2016. I was supposed to go see Rah. My mother's car wasn't that good, but she had my back in anything, so we were on our way to.

It had been a week since I had heard from Rah. I was so confused. I was calling his counselor in prison to see if he was okay and, when I found out he was, I was confused as to why he wasn't calling me or writing me. That's when I received a letter in the mail from Rah, and I was excited. I hadn't heard from him, so I was just happy to know that he was okay.

When I opened the letter, I was taken aback. Rah was calling me every liar in the book and telling me how he had called off his engagement with Larissa because of how she had done me. Engagement? I was completely lost at this point because he'd told me that they were never engaged. He told me they weren't even together, and that he had never met her before. So, all of a sudden, they were engaged?

Rah was upset because I had posted the balloons and flowers that he'd gotten me for my birthday, and Larissa saw them. Bony screen shot my page and sent the pictures to Rah, telling him that I was taunting Larissa. I couldn't understand how I could taunt a bitch I didn't give a fuck about.

I called Shawna, crying my eyes out. The only thing she did was remain silent. I thought she was just allowing me to vent my pains away, but little did I know was that she was glad. She was glad that I was hurting.

"You hurt her, that's why she's targeting you on Facebook."

"How did I hurt her? Rah lied, not me!" I screamed.

"I don't like Larissa, but I understand her. I'm in her shoes. You're April and I'm Larissa. We know that our men are dealing with other women and we have to accept that. We have to deal with seeing yawl broadcast yawl relationship with our men. We have to deal with the fact that our men are dealing with other women and catching feelings for yawl."

When Shawna said that, I knew the bitch was bat shit crazy. Larissa had no right to target me the way that she did, and Rah had no right to disrespect me the way he did. Later that night, Shawna had called me to tell me to check Facebook. I did and saw that Larissa had posted that her and Rah had gotten engaged. I knew it was true because his aunt commented on the photo, so I knew there was no denying it.

I had completely shut down. I was broken. I felt stupid. I looked stupid. I was stupid. I vented on Facebook and, once again, Dollar Bill couldn't just let me handle my pain my way. He had to hit me up, making it about him and Shawna.

Dollar Bill: *Gm when you awake. I see posts of yours that make me think you're talking about Shawna. If so, that would be wrong. People have your back, but you should never expect them to compromise who they are in showing it. All things dealing with Rah is your personal life.*

Nobody wants to get involved in that bcuz they can fall out with people and he can call you up and you'll go right back to him. I'm very disappointed in how you're handling this. You almost sounded like you're ready to distance yourself from BTB last night. I don't want you to do that, but I don't want you with BTB if you don't want to be here. I've fought for you every step of the way. But I will allow you to do what will make you happy. But your contract would revert back to Spider. Reds, when you act like this, it feels like spit in my face for all of my efforts, understanding, and compromise. You should be concentrating on writing. This is very draining and, in all honesty, Rah was never really yours. Bcuz had he been yours, he wouldn't have cared if you screamed it to the world.

Me: *Gm, and none of my posts are about Shawna. I could easily have a phone conversation with her if I had a problem. I don't understand why everyone thinks I'm bitch made to the point I have to be indirect.*

& Whether you, Shawna, God, or anyone else don't believe me, I KNOW ME. And once you disrespect me, ain't no coming back. I'm done with him. So, he can't just call me up and things go back to normal. & I never said anything about leaving or wanting to leave. Am I going to stay to myself? Yea I am. & You don't have to tell me that because I'm already aware.

Dollar Bill: *It's cool then. I will let you do it your way. I'm here if you need me.*

Me: *I'm going to stay to myself. I'm not interested in building relationships or friendships with anyone else. I honestly don't know how you can be disappointed in me when I haven't done anything. People can say what they want about me but, the moment I even think about clapping back, I'm wrong? I don't get it. I'm human too. In every situation I'm in, I get blamed. I take responsibility for my actions and, yet, that's still not enough. Which is why I have this idgaf attitude. Yes, I was upset, and I'm still upset. But just because you and others have* different views on the situation, don't make me feel like I'm wrong. I feel like I'm intentionally being hurt by the fact that he wasn't really my man to begin with constantly being thrown in my face, as if I didn't know. I do have feelings at times. No one knows me or what I go through, personally. I'm big on respect. That's all I got left, and I'm not letting no one take that away from me.

Dollar Bill: Reds, it's cool. I've always supported you, always told you the truth, always gave you the best advice I could. Tried to be a friend, etc. I hope that's been good enough. But you make me feel it hasn't. Bcuz when you go against my advice and it turns out bad, you still feel I let you down. A true friend doesn't mind hurting your feelings if it helps you to grow.

Me: I didn't say you let me down. I just felt like in this situation I was looked at as a liar and I know I'm not one. And I thought since you knew too, then the situation wouldn't have been so hurtful for me. But it *is what it is. What happened happened, and I can't change it. Actually, I don't want to because I got the truth this way.*

Dollar Bill was right; if Rah was really mine, he wouldn't mind me putting it out there. I couldn't deny the fact that I was hurt. I was broken. Everything I touched or loved went up in shambles. It was my stupidity to fall for a nigga in prison, but he had no right to play me the way he did. My career was already on the line, and I never asked him for money or anything of that nature. All I asked was for him to not make me look stupid because I had a career to worry about.

43

True Colors

I**T WAS WHINING DOWN TO ME REALIZING EVEN MORE** that I just wasn't getting anywhere with Behind The Bars Publications. What hurt me the most was when Dollar Bill promoted him and Shawna's upcoming release the day that my book *She Don't Deserve The Dick* was released. Then, after us discussing that my book would be two ninety-nine, he had the nerve to put it up for ninety-nine cents. As much as I tried to bite my tongue, I couldn't. I had to say something because I knew for a fact that he was trying to be disrespectful.

Me: *Do you think that will take people's attention off my book since you posting yours.*

Dollar Bill: *Nah, I'ma come back with yours. Mine don't even drop until the 28th.*

An author should post about their books every day.

His response was a bunch of bullshit, and I knew it was bullshit. I didn't respond until the next day when I noticed the price of my book.

Me: *My book is live. I thought it was supposed to be 2.99?*

Dollar Bill: *We thought it over. We'll change it to $2.99 once I see the initial rankings.*

Me: *Who is we?*

Dollar Bill: *We is always me and Shawna. She is the COO. But, thinking about it, I don't wanna raise it to $2.99. If the response to it is good, in number of sales, you'll kill em with book 2. The difference in .99 and $2.99 will only equate to $100-$150 bcuz most will use kindle unlimited for a $2.99 book anyway. So, our concern should be more readers over $100.*

When I read his message, I was pissed. I hated how he thought he had such a business-like mind. I mean, if that was the case, his company wouldn't have been going downhill the way it was. He always tried to make it seem like it was just business, but I knew he was doing certain shit on purpose.

There was rarely any compromising when it came to me and Dollar Bill. I would always try to give my input on things, but he would always overpower me. Like, it was either his way or the highway.

Dollar Bill: *Now you're in your feelings and not responding to your readers who bought the book. This is why you're having trouble getting back on top. But today I'm through babying you. From this point on you're going to have to be professional. I'm not giving no more breaks, none. I'm changing the price of your book and whatever happens, happens. It's all business now, straight business*

Me: *I don't have anything to say. & I'm really not trying to hear none of that. I'm so sick of that bullshit. I heard it from Spider, and now you. Don't keep blaming me for me not so called being on top. Release me! I keep trying and trying but fuck it. This right here shows me you don't believe in me. All that bullshit about you believe in me but can't* *even price my book for what it's worth. Then you gon discuss it with Shawna like she actually gives a flying fuck! I been keeping ma mouth shut and I'm sick of it. Yawl got me fucked up if you think I'ma sit back and let yawl continue to play me. I'm not making shit. Every fucking time I look I gotta come to you about money. That shouldn't be happening. I'm making chump change. And you expect me to keep giving you books? I bust my ass making sure I meet the word count. Making sure my story is on point and you gon place that shit for .99 cents? Keep it real it's because you don't believe in me. You might as well release me outta the contract and make whatever threats you gon back. And you can screenshot this and send it to Shawna since I mentioned her because yawl about to feel the wrath.*

Dollar Bill: *I'm not going to argue. Do what you feel is best*

Me: NO! *You wrote me so we gon finish this. I swear if I would have known that I would go through this I would have never* got in this industry. After Spider I would've been done for good. Yawl not gon keep coming at me stupid. I may not know the industry, but I observe a lot and you gotta fight for ya respect. Every time I look I gotta bow down to the readers. NO! Not when I'm bustin out 50k to 55k word books! Either they buy it or they don't. Then as soon as I ask to borrow some money I gotta hear "Ooh I just hate how people always going to him for money" well if I was making some I wouldn't ask. Don't make no sense. I keep calm and I stay to myself but I be damned if I keep being quiet when it's some fuckery going on.

Dollar Bill: *Reds did Shawna say that to you? Anyway, queen, just calm down. I'm gonna change the price of your book. Man, the book ain't been out 5 hours and YOU'RE already fighting about it. Relax. I didn't give you my money to pay your phone bill. I advanced you yours. Man, you driving me crazy.*

Me: *This isn't about the price. It's about YOU believing in me how you say you do! Take risks and you ain't about taking risks. Or risk or whatever the hell the word is. Whether the readers buy it or not, it still shows that you believe in me and where I can go. I'm not gon hit best seller overnight. I done already came to terms that that's gon take time. Ya main focus is me hitting best sellers whether it's for me or the company idk, but I know that's what you focused on. And because of that you making sure you please the readers as much as you can. And Shawna said more than that to me. Like I said I've been biting my tongue a lot because everybody and they mama in this industry got a story about me. But we ain't cool no more for no reason.*

Dollar Bill read my Facebook message and came at me with more excuses. I knew they were excuses, but I made him think that I was willing to compromise when, in all reality, I really wasn't. I was mentally drained. I had a bad habit of breaking down whether I was angry or sad. I become extremely emotional. I tried to give him the benefit of the doubt once again, but the disrespect continued, which resulted in another verbal altercation.

Me: *I noticed you ain't really post or push my book like that.*

And don't say that I'm driving you crazy and starting because I'm not. But I am going to speak my mind from now on. The only person that promoted for me was Sharon Bel. Of course, people shared it and such. Maybe three people from BTB changed their covers. Shawna posted in one group for me. And now you right back talking about your book, which people are looking forward to. You pumped Bre and Rah up for some reason. I'm just tryna see if this is how you and Shawna gon move from now on so I can do what I need to do.

Dollar Bill: *That's not true. Missy promoted your book. I asked you to find a promoter and you chose Sharon. I pay her, so that's me promoting for you. You keep throwing Shawna name up. She's writing, and I don't have to apologize for promoting* *my own book on my own page. I posted yours on my page this mooring. Now straight up, Reds, you're gonna have to miss me with the drama and do like I do, go hard on your own page. You're still posting negative post over there, don't no reader wanna see all that. They have enough of that in their own lives. If you no longer wanna be a part of BTB and the new move. Give me NTARB3 and I keep your royalties until your debt is paid. I'll release you from your contract after you turn in NTARB3. I told you I'm not going through this with you no more. It's your decision to make. I'm tryna reach the top and I don't need this negative stuff in my life. If you can do it better than me, good luck.*

Me: *It's so funny how when I speak up, I'm drama. So then let it be drama. I'm not friends with Missy, but I saw exactly who she was promoting, and it wasn't me. I chose Sharon Bel because she was cheap, and I tried to be reasonable. And I'll post what I want. Yawl want me to keep things on hush*

hush. I honestly see why people left BTB. And what makes it so bad is that I'm referring people to yawl and I shouldn't be. As far as Shawna, please don't make it seem like I can't call her up. I'm not Strawberry and I'm really trying to be professional and keep things to a minimum. But ya responses and the way you come at me is crazy. And of course, you would throw money in there. The same thing Rocky and Spider did. Kept my money thinking that would break me. Dollar, you ain't no different. You fed me good words just to get me over here and yawl took me through the same bullshit. I'm not writing anything. Take me to court. If I can't come to you about the way I'm feeling then, yea, we ain't got nothing else to talk about

Dollar Bill: *I'm not tryna break you. You seem unhappy and you're hurting my energy with your constant negative attitude. I don't wish to take your money. I'm just saying I wish to be repaid the money you owe me, then your free to go. If you don't* *want to write anything else, fine. I'll take the loss and charge it to the game. I'll keep whatever royalties come on from the books you already gave me until I'm paid off. After that, you'll get your royalties. No hard feelings. I tried very hard with you. It just may be time for us to part ways. I wish you the best tho.*

Me: *You used me just like Spider did. Ain't no way I've been with you for a year and I'm not making anything. You thought I wouldn't peep game. Don't try to play victim. You don't wanna hear the truth about your company, but yawl crossed the wrong one. I'm very unhappy with BTB and I told you why but because it's ya bread and butter you ain't tryna hear shit from the many people that complained. You doing exactly what you intended to do, which is why you still keep in contact with Spider. Yawl was shady from jump and I was too stupid to see. Don't wish me the best at all. All that shit is fake. You chose to pay for that lawyer after I said NO. You chose to pay*

Rocky after I said NO. Those were your choices, NOT MINES.

Dollar Bill: *Reds, we made an agreement, and I have it documented, that you would repay what I spent getting you out of those contracts. I never used you, it's just that you're becoming too combative. Every day it's something different. I don't care about what happened in your personal relationship with Shawna. It has no effect on my decisions. Just take a second to think about this. You've had a problem with 3 different publishers. Maybe one or two of them was wrong, but I know I wasn't. I gave you all the support I could. You're just impatient. Your writing and editing was much better with BTB. You didn't see the financial success you wanted but that was gonna come. When you calm down and think about it, you'll see that I was never against you. The way you're acting now and the things you're thinking of doing is straight wrong for you to do to me. You're unhappy so I'm releasing you with no fight.*

Oh, and I'm never a victim. I took a chance on you bcuz I believed in you. I thought that if I showed you love, you would get back on top and silence the haters. You've turned against me tho. Still, I'm never a victim bcuz no one forced me to trust in you. But, I've learned a valuable lesson. So, I thank you for that. Please take care

Me: *I'm done with this conversation. I honestly don't care what you have documented. I remember the conversations we had, and I said I was done with writing and I didn't want to be signed with you. But your words "you're too talented to let someone take your passion away from you". And there you go maybe one or two of them was wrong. So, I'm guessing Levi trying to fuck me was so right. I'm guessing Spider tryna fuck me and my mother was so right. I'm guessing him lying on me was so right. And it does affect you. I done heard the stories. I kept ma mouth shut each time Shawna belittled me. I confided in her and thought that she was a good person and,* considering I had no relationship with my own sisters, she could be that one. But looking down on me because I had an STD is disrespectful. Running ya mouth to Kim about me and Rah is disloyal. Acting so fuckin innocent but you low-key messy and an instigator. You hurt? Then so be it. Now you feel how I feel. I was broken when I came to yawl and yawl used that against me. I had just gotten out of the hospital from ma ex whoopin ma ass and giving me several std's, on top of going through what Spider was taking me through. I trusted you just enough. You sold me the same dreams he did. I was repping BTB hard. Nay even said that I would no longer feel the same way about BTB once I was here for a while. I told him to shove it and stop being miserable. And I ain't turn against you. I fell back. After I saw how you did me after Rah did me dirty, I fell back. I'm not disloyal. That don't run through my blood. I'm not gon call the prison or no shit like that. That ain't how I roll. I came to you as a woman, regardless if *you felt like it was drama or not. I told you how I felt and yawl pick and choose who yawl support heavy. Now you need to think about that*

Dollar Bill: *You keep talking about Shawna and y'all personal relationship, which has nothin to do with me and BTB business. This right here is where you always run from the hard truth. If Shawna talked behind your back, who told her your business? YOU DID. So that's where you must accept the blame yourself. Nay is on his own and how is his books selling? They're not! You haven't told me nothing I did wrong to you yet. And if you think I support one author over the next, that's crazy. I want everybody book to sell bcuz it increases the profit. You want me to be mad at Rah? Nah, I'm mad at you bcuz I told you to leave him alone, but YOU didn't listen. Again, that's on YOU. You lash out at me bcuz I'm the closest one for you to lash out at. You got something to say to Shawna? Inbox her like you're doing me. I always told you the truth, but*

I'm not babying you. You already have enough of that and it's detrimental, even if it's done out of love. Please don't inbox me again unless it's something positive bcuz I'm not responding to anymore mess

Me: *I explained the situation to you. Whether you would want to hear it or not. And I sure do take the blame for disclosing my business. And I don't have anything to say to her. You're the CEO, so I'm coming to you. But you done with the conversation and so am I. You gon continue to lose authors so, if you like it, I love it.*

I was hurt, and I was angry after the conversation me and Dollar Bill had. Here I was, putting just a little bit of trust in another man, and getting nothing but shit in return. I knew that it was my fault for getting involved in yet another bullshit ass contract. In my mind, I was fighting for my career, no matter what but, in the eyes of these publishers, I was just another problem author. The next day, Dollar Bill hit me up, and I honestly thought that I had broken something in him for him to stop doing me dirty.

Dollar Bill: *Reds, I took a minute to really try to understand your anger. I won't claim to know the hurt you've been through with the abuse, bullying, ridicule, name calling, and all the other things you've had to deal with in your young life. I've faced my own troubles, but they weren't anything like yours. See, I've always been successful in my endeavors popular and well liked. So, I can't truly understand your pain. I wish there was a way I could wash it all away, but I can't. What I do know is that you have been scarred. I'm sorry those things happened to you. I'm also sorry I was never able to gain your trust. I hope one day you're able to fully overcome those demons. That's straight from my heart*

Me: *I'm not perfect. I know my attitude sucks and I can be ignorant at times. Well, a lot of times. But I'm really a good person and I've been burned a lot, so I have a major wall up. That's maybe why I've been clashing with you because you didn't experience what I have. But after talking to my mother, I* realize that you haven't done anything to me personally. I apologize if I said anything that hurt you. I'm not used to succeeding in anything so, with this author stuff, I'm fighting hard for it. But it seems like I'm fighting the wrong people. I don't want to stop writing. I'm tired of giving up and I don't want to do that anymore. If we can start over and just keep pushing forward, I would really like that. You can change the books price back to .99 cents. From now on, I won't focus on the price, and I'll just understand that every move is to make my fanbase stronger. I do want to thank you for everything. Even though I keep pushing you away. You still seem to keep fighting for me and holding me down, even when at times I don't deserve it.

Dollar Bill: *Ok queen. I believe that would make things better. Just try to have some patience. We'll discuss a game plan in detail once I finish this book and take a few days to breath.*

Things didn't get easier after that conversation. I thought I was doing the right thing by trying to see the bigger picture. I felt like maybe I was tripping a little. But, the more I tried to put those thoughts in my head, the more I realized that my gut was right from the beginning. No matter how much I tried to see if Dollar Bill had a little good in him, I was always proved wrong. He was just as evil as they came, but what could one expect? After spending almost twenty-five years in prison. Manipulation is something he mastered and, I couldn't front, he had me feeling like I was in a dangerous game of tug of war. Only I was being tugged by stupid on one side and truth on the other.

44

Sick and Tired of Being Sick and Tired

I WAS LASHING OUT A LOT MORE BECAUSE I WAS SEEING just how shady and grimy Behind The Bars publications really was, and the COO Shawna was on the verge of getting her ass whooped. I was so angry so, instead of tagging Dollar Bill and Shawna like I wanted to, I would update an indirect status that hit a nerve to anyone that was guilty.

Every time I would post something on Facebook, Dollar Bill would hit me up and criticize me. I was tired of not being able to express myself without there being a problem. At this point, I was done. I was tired. I just couldn't hold in my frustrations any longer. I was so sick of being looked at as the problem, when I knew that I hadn't done anything wrong. On top of that, Shawna had been sending me screenshots of Bonni and Larissa's post about how they were planning on putting hands on me if I came to the book event.

Their plans were to jump me at the Harlem Book Fair, all over a nigga in prison. A nigga that had been with me for almost a year and didn't claim her until he found out that I had posted the flowers and balloons he sent me for my birthday on Facebook. They wanted to take it further than Facebook, and I was okay with that. I was tired of being bullied on Facebook, and I was ready to show these bitches why I didn't do the talking. I was a trained to go killer. I was silent for a reason. Wasn't no bitch in my blood, and I was ready to tear they asses up at that book event. I no longer cared about my career. I was fed up to the max but, no matter how fed up I was, my mother was not about to let me risk the rest of my career over some bum ass authors who didn't have shit going for themselves but drama.

"I'm not going to allow you to go to New York and be fighting. If they were really bout it, they would pull up to ya crib like they said they was. Don't show out at a book event. That's what they want you to do. They want to continue to make you look bad. You're way better than that. Those girls are in their late thirties messing with a twenty-two-year-old. That ain't nothing but jealousy. She need to check that nigga that's in prison. Because he's the one that lied. Don't stoop to their level. Let them continue to talk. Ain't no bitch putting their hands on you," she said.

I listened to my mother's words and let them marinate. It took me some time to realize and understand what she meant. So, I decided not to go to the Harlem Book Fair that year because although I knew it wasn't worth, the moment I saw them, it was going to be an all-out brawl.

But, even though I was the one being threatened, Dollar Bill still came at me sideways and I recalled our last conversation being very unfriendly.

Dollar Bill: *I see your posts and, again, you're back to that, always putting your business out there when people have shown they don't care. You can call Aniya up and tell her that, since she's the only one commenting. I'm not mad tho. This is just who you are. Do what you have to do and I'ma do the same. It's straight business from this point forward, no hard feelings.*

Me: *I'm really trying to keep things professional Dollar Bill. Not once have I disrespected you. But yet, you keep coming at me and I'm tired of it. I don't give a fuck who cares about my post. IT'S MY PAGE! Like, why the hell are you so pressed?! No one is trying to make you mad. I came to you as a woman. You got in your feelings and that's not my problem. Point blank period, I'm not getting anywhere with Behind The Bars Publications. But, all in all, I'm not trying to leave. Just trying to branch out for more exposure. But, that's a fuckin crime I see. If it's not Shawna or Rah. You not rocking hard with them or supporting them. I always gotta be the one to keep ma fuckin mouth shut. I swear on ma mother's life and ma dead baby life. One of yawl got one more time to come at me and I'ma snap the fuck out. Because I ain't did shit. Here you are in ma fuckin inbox about a post on ma page. But ya best friend Bony and Larissa talking about they gon see me at the Harlem book* *fair. This why I barely deal with people from BTB now.*

Dollar Bill: *I'm done.*

Me: *Be done Dollar Bill, I don't care. You wanted to be done, which is why you started with me. You and Rah gon get exactly what's coming to yawl because I'm tired of yawl fuckin with me and makin threats, when I haven't done shit. And please get Shawna involved because I'm just waiting to beat her the fuck up. My sisters is ready believe that shit. Yawl not gon keep using me and talkin shit like I'm not gon do shit in return.*

Dollar Bill: *Recently, it has come to my attention that you plan to release books outside of Behind The Bars Publications, which would violate your contract. We will not permit you to do THAT, until your contract terms with Behind The Bars Publications has been fulfilled or we have reached a mutual decision to terminate the contract.*

I will send you an itemized list of advance money you owe and any loans and charges for book covers we purchased for you, for stories you have failed to turn in.

Once you have repaid those debts AND you have turned in the finale of NTARB, we will gladly release you from further terms of your contract.

Absent of your compliance with the aforementioned terms, Behind The Bars Publications will oppose any books you attempt to publish with any other company, independently, and under any other alias or pseudonym.

You will receive a formal document listing what you owe and restating what I've said in this message.

My hope is that we will solve our differences amicably.

Best wishes

I never responded to his message. There wasn't even supposed to be a *Never Trust A Ratchet Bitch* part three. I couldn't understand how he kept telling me that my books weren't selling but constantly harassing me for a book that I was never supposed to write to begin with. I knew that Dollar Bill was just trying to do any and everything in his power to break me. He was upset that I had plans on moving on and that I wanted more.

From day one, he preyed on me; he watched my every move and, when it was his time to attack, he did. I couldn't blame him for taking my insecurities and using them against me. I even got the publishing company tatted on me because he said that it would show my loyalty. I was at a very weak point in my life. I had been fighting battle after battle, and he figured that I would be too weak to fight with him.

45

Sick and Tired of Being Sick and Tired

THERE WERE TIMES WHERE I WOULD JUST BE CHILLING, staying off of social media, just to get my thoughts right and try to figure out a game plan. My mother was struggling and stressing, and I was stressing watching her struggle. Writing books was my passion, but it was also a way out of the hood. It was supposed to open many doors for me, but the stress that came with it had me giving up. No matter how much I tried to take a step back to figure shit out, Dollar Bill would find his way in my inbox talking shit.

Dollar Bill: *Every day it's something different and it's getting tiresome bcuz when you asked for covers to motivate you, advances or whatever, I did it w/o question. Now, you're ready to bail out. If you would* listen to me concerning the things you post on social media, I'm convinced your career would bounce back. You say you're not concerned with what people think, well you shouldn't be concerned with sales. You gotta promote and you gotta be interactive with readers. I'm gonna set up some online interviews for you. But, you have to do your part. You haven't said anything about your edits or anything. I can't set a release date w/o knowing when you'll be done with them. And you should want to have as long as possible to promote the release. In order to get better results, you have to change what isn't working.

Me: *I haven't started the edits yet, but they'll get done.*

Dollar Bill: *It seems that you no longer have the passion. I'm just going to wait for you to regain it.*

Me: *I don't, but I'ma get the books done regardless.*

Dollar Bill: *I'm not gonna sweat it anymore. Basically, you just had me waste* money on covers and editing and promotions and everything else. Gave me a fake friendship and all of that. But, I'ma take that lesson and learn from it, and I'ma make this move and help the authors that wanna be with BTB prosper. I'm not even mad. If you're not actively promoting and interacting, the book will fail anyway. So, if I don't see you doing any of that, I'm not going to release it anyway. I'll probably have to tell Spider we can't fulfill the contract

Me: *Are you threatening me with Spider? I really hope that's not what you're doing. Because I can give two fucks about Spider. If the contract reverts back to him, he's shit out of luck because he will never receive his books. I have a lawyer, so he can take me to court if he wants. I said I was going to get the books done. I promote when I can or when I'm not blocked. If you need to, take the money that you spent on everything out of what I make. I'm not understanding where all this is coming from and why you always* on me, when there are other authors on BTB who don't do anything. All they do is release a book and it takes them forever to do that.

Dollar Bill: *No threat. If you know Spider, you know he contacts me every month about this. I've had to argue with him about you every month. But, I don't wanna stress over this anymore. I'm going to write. Just find your place and holla at me when your thoughts are clearer. And I'm on you because you have more potential than the others, but you're allowing these tough times to kill your determination. And you're wearing me out. I need you to believe in yourself like I believe in you.*

Me: *You shouldn't have to argue with him over me. If it's that much, release me, but he will never get another book out of me, so everyone will be screwed. And he probably only contacts you about money because that's all he's about.*

Dollar Bill was sneaky. Now, I understood why him and Shawna got along so well. They were both out to destroy. Even after me and Rah were done,

Dollar Bill was still contacting me, letting me know that Rah said hello or that he missed me.

46

The First Step Is To Admit: The Road to Closure

IT TOOK ME A LONG TIME TO ADMIT THAT I WAS depressed, unhappy, sad, hurt, confused, and full of pain. For the last 4-5 years, I had been depressed. Depressed because I was constantly fighting a losing battle. Depressed because everything I loved, I lost. Depressed because I had two older sisters that didn't love me, and I was out here in the cold world learning what life was really like on my own. Depressed because I didn't feel loved.

Depressed because every guy I came across hurt me. Depressed because I continuously blamed myself for my rape. Depressed because I had a passion for writing but, no matter how much I fought, it seemed like I was getting nowhere. Depressed because I constantly witnessed pain in my mother's eyes, but there was nothing I could do to fix it. Depressed because I was loyal to females who I thought were my friends, but they ended up being the enemy.

Depressed because I KNEW that I was a good person, but the way I was treated made me feel like I wasn't. I blamed myself constantly for being mistreated. I blamed myself constantly for people not liking me. I blamed myself constantly for the wrongdoings that were done to me. I blamed myself constantly for all the pain and hurt I endured. So, in order to not feel the pain anymore, I cut myself. It felt good to feel pain but not feel it. Cutting was my way of healing. Cutting was my way of not feeling the physical and mental pain that I was actually feeling. I cut myself until I felt numb. It was easy for people to judge me but walking in my shoes? Nah, they couldn't do that.

47

The Fight: The Last Straw

A FEW DECEMBERS BACK, I GOT INTO A REAL BAD altercation with my big sister Dani. My mother was venting on Facebook about how unhappy she was, and the shit made me mad. I got on her status and let her know that she needed to stop the crying shit and remove those who were hurting her out of her life. I was tired of giving my mother soft love. She needed tough love so that she could understand exactly what I meant. Apparently, Dani saw the status and she must've wanted some attention because she commented running her mouth.

"Dani, ain't nobody thinking about you or talking to you."

"Nunni, watch your mouth because you know how I am."

"And Dani, you know how I am. So, what you sayin'?"

"I pull up and you know that."

"Pull up, I'm at Nanny's."

At this time, we were homeless again and we were staying with my father's mother. I couldn't stand her ass and, as much as I tried to give her chance after chance, she proved to me each time how she was a bitter, conniving old person.

I was on the phone with Aniya when Dani pulled up. I was sitting on the couch waiting for her to come in.

"Dad, answer the door. Dani here and she wants to fight."

"What? Look, don't bring that shit here. This is why I didn't want ya ass to come back in the first place," he said while opening the door.

As soon as he did, Dani came in with sneakers and jeans on, so I already knew what type of time she was on.

"Nunni, I'm tell ya fat, dirty ass this one time-"

That was all she needed to say before I got up and cracked her in her shit. I had socks on, so I slipped on the carpet and, the whole time, my dad was between us. She had my hoodie, and I had her shirt. I lifted myself up and, as I did, I grabbed a glass bottle vase. I was fat and my arms were short so, when it came to fighting, I fought dirty. I went back as far as I could and, when I brought my hand back down, I smashed her in the head with the bottle vase.

After that, I rammed her into the wall, and she was trying to push me away, but the rage in me overpowered him. I was stomping Dani out and, when I couldn't throw any more punches, I picked up picture frames and smashed them on top of her head. In order to separate us, my dad had to tell his mom to get his taser.

That brought me back to reality because I calmed down just a little, which allowed Dani to get up and, when she did, she smacked me in my face.

"Nunni, move so I can get Dani out of the house."

I took a step back and picked up a table and tried to throw it at her, but my dad caught it.

"You miserable, fat, dirty bitch! She's mad because no dude gon' ever want her fat ugly ass. Her books not selling, and her fat ass is homeless. You miserable bitch!" Dani yelled.

When it was all said and done, my mother was called and the blame was put on me. She cursed me out, and I was put out of my grandmother's house. That wasn't nothing new though. Ain't nobody fuck with me from jump.

***

After having nothing but bad experiences in Jersey, I felt like it was time for a change. Not to mention, after the altercation I had been staying with my brother's baby mom, and I went from being happy, losing weight to being stressed the hell out and back to gaining weight because of her current boyfriend making sure I was miserable there.

He made my life there a living hell. Whatever cup I drunk out of, he would throw it in the trash. He complained about them having to feed an extra person, which resulted in me not eating at all. My mother thought I was losing weight because I was finally happy, but she had no clue that I was stressing and not eating.

I knew that it was time for me to make moves when I saw my nephew get his ass beat so bad that his lip was busted and his tooth was knocked out. There was no reason for him to be beat like that but, I realized that in order to get to me, they had to hurt him because we were so close.

I had just gotten finished ordering Burger King when me and my mother were sitting in the parking lot. I had just text Aniya and told her to call me, which she did in seconds.

"Hey sis, I need a favor."

"Wassup boo?"

"I need to know if you're willing to let me stay with you, just until I can get on my feet. I don't get much from my books, but I'm willing to give you all the money I get if you let me stay with you.

"Nah, we not gonna do all that. We'll just do a back and forth thing, so nobody here would get tired of you," she said.

That was all that needed to be said because my mother scraped up money and used her last to get me to New York that same weekend.

48

Friend or Foe: The Beginning of the End Of A Toxic Friendship

ANIYA WAS A BESTSELLING AUTHOR AS WELL. WE HAD our rocky moments when we were signed to Praise & Glory Publications, but we ended up squashing that beef and working on building a friendship. I genuinely loved Aniya. I supported her in everything she did, defended her when someone spoke bad about her, and listened to her whenever she needed a shoulder.

I admired Aniya. She had an entire family but, yet, she still managed to write and put books out back to back. She would always tell me that no matter where she went, she was taking me with her because I was her lil sis, and that made me feel good that someone actually cared about me. I wasn't close to my real big sisters, so to have someone that cared about me that much meant a lot.

I would always support Aniya more than I did myself. I would share her book links, promote her books for her, encourage her authors because she was also a publisher, and listen to her whenever she was going through something. Whenever she felt like she was done with the industry, I would tell her to fuck the haters and keep spitting out those bangers. I was riding with her one thousand percent.

But, no matter how much I was showing her that I loved her and I supported her, I never really got it in return. She was always hesitant to support me the way I supported her. She would rarely share my book links, and she would always give me the runaround when it came to us doing a collab together. Time and time again, I let what was being shown to me slide. I let it slide until it was too late.

49

He Loves Me, He Loves Me Not

DEW WAS MY EVERYTHING. I WAS SO IN LOVE WITH THAT man but I knew, deep down, he didn't give a damn about me. I was praying and hoping that, someday, he would see how good of a person I was and finally show me the same interest back.

While I was in New York, I kept in contact with him. That was something I always did, but mainly just to see how his attitude was considering there was a possibility I could've been pregnant and with his child.

I remember it like it was yesterday. I was at the laundromat with Aniya and her husband. They were doing laundry and so was I. I had just put my clothes in the washer and I was now sitting on the bench. My phone started ringing and I got a funny feeling in my stomach because the call was coming from Dew, but it was from the same phone he said he lost, so I already knew it was some bullshit.

"Hello?" I answered.

"Talk to her. You wanted to call her so bad so talk to her," Dew said in the background.

"Who are you to Dew?" she asked me.

"Who did he say I was?" I replied.

"Tell me who you are?" she asked again.

"Me and Dew been dealing for two years now. I don't see him often but, when I do, we fuck and we don't use condoms," I told her.

I was aggravated by now because I hated confrontation.

"What? Are you fucking serious? Well, I'm his wife; Dew has been married for five years!" she said.

"What? Nah, Dew isn't married. I know him. He's not married. If that's the case, we wouldn't have been dealing for two years," I said.

"Yo, you lyin'! You know I ain't never fuck you! I ain't never wanted to fuck wit' you!" Dew yelled into the phone.

"Really Dew! I'm lying now? Matter of fact, hold on," I said and clicked over.

By this time, I was calling my mother. She was all up and through me and Dew's relationship, so she knew what was up.

"This is my mother on the phone. She knows me and Dew was dealing," I mentioned.

"Woooowww. So, you know her mother, Dew? You know her mother?"

"Man, look, you wanted the truth, so you got it. Yea, I fucked with her. You happy? What you gon' do with the information you got?" he asked.

I was balled up by now. In tears, I could barely breath, and I wasn't home with my mother for comfort. I wanted to die. It felt like all the oxygen had been sucked from my body.

***

When we got home, Aniya was in her room folding clothes and cleaning up. I was on the phone with one of my gamer friends and he was trying his best to help me get through. I knew there was nothing he could do to help me and, after a while, I really didn't want to talk anymore. I was sitting in the dark trying to get my mind right, when Aniya walked in and told me to come in her room.

"What's going on sis?" she asked.

"Earlier when we went out to fill out job applications, I text Dew just to let him know what I was doing because before I left Jersey, I told him I would update him on how I was doing. When I did text him, I knew that the texts were coming back funny. I asked him what was wrong, and he said he had a headache. I believed him because I knew he suffered from them. But then, I get a call and he cussing me out saying don't text that number no more, but then I get a call while we at the laundromat and it's a female saying she his wife. Like, after two years of us dealing, you got a whole wife?"

I went on and on crying and venting while Aniya continued to fold her clothes. I could see her body language that she didn't really care about the things I was saying. Did it bother me? Yes, but I couldn't blame her because she wasn't an emotional person like I was.

"Can I speak now?" she asked.

I nodded my head yes.

"Now, you know I'm ya sis and I'ma keep it real with you regardless. The truth was there, you just decided not to see it. In so many words, he was telling you that he wasn't shit and that he did have someone. He kept saying he was going to hurt you and fuck ya life up. That was enough right there," she said.

I felt her on what she was saying. I wasn't mad at that because as I thought about it, he was trying to tell me the truth and what he was about just in his own way and his own words.

"You right and I get that, but I'm not going to sit here and act like I deserved for him to hurt me," I told her.

"In so many ways, you brought it on yourself, and this is why I say I never want to fall in love or be in love with a man because I don't want to feel or look like you do right now," she told me.

That night, me, Aniya, and her husband had some drinks and had a good time. She didn't want me to be down, nor did she want me to think about that fuck nigga. I was so thankful for them because my mind was set to go in depression mode.

"My wife done had a lot of females stop being friends with her. She done had drama with a lot of females, and I try to prevent it at times, but she don't listen. I've been feeling you out since you been here, and I like you. I see you love my wife, and I see that you're real. I like that, and I know my wife likes that because if she didn't, then you wouldn't be here," he said.

I sat back and listened to him. He was speaking some real shit, but it also made me a bit nervous when he said that Aniya had a falling out with a lot of females. It made me question why? Why couldn't she get a long with females?

"So, what about Terry?" I asked.

"I don't rock with her like that, and she ain't never been in my house before either," she said.

"Fareal?" I asked in a bit of a shock.

"I'm dead ass. I don't rock with her like that and, if I don't trust you like that, then I'm damn sure not gon' bring you into my house. Each time she came by here, she waited outside. Even when she brought me those chocolate covered strawberries she didn't step foot in my house. I trust you, which is why you're in my house. Around my kids and my husband," Aniya told me.

It felt good to know that Aniya trusted me, but I still questioned why every female she came across she was no longer friends with. I knew that I didn't have friends and that I was crossed but, for some reason, I felt weary when I heard that.

50

Friend or Foe: The Beginning of the End of A Toxic Friendship

ANIYA WELCOMED ME INTO HER HOME. I WAS SO thankful because I had to get away from Jersey. I needed a change and a new environment, so moving there was a breath of fresh air. Everything was good at first; we were going out, staying up late at night, writing, gossiping, and just living life. I was happy, semi stress free, and just ready for whatever change was going to come.

However, although things were going good at first, things slowly but surely started to unravel right before my eyes about a month later.

"Can I talk to you?" Aniya asked.

"Yea," I told her.

I followed her into her bedroom and closed the door.

"Wassup?" I asked.

"You know if I had the extra space, you could stay here forever, but I don't. The kids have been going crazy, and my daughter told my husband how she overheard you on the phone talking about sex," she explained.

I was confused. Because she knew she didn't have the extra space from jump, so where was all of this coming from? I had no clue. Then, on top of that, her daughter lied? Why? I still had no clue.

"That's not true. I watch how I talk because I share a room with your girls. So, why would she say that? This is crazy. I hate to be lied on, and now I have to leave because of a lie," I responded.

"Sis, no, you don't have to leave because of that. My husband knows when his daughter is lying. He's just overprotective of her, whether she's a liar or not. I just don't have the extra space. So, we can go to the shelter tomorrow," she said.

I was hurt, but I didn't express it. I responded with a simple nod before walking out. I went back into Alana's room and her oldest daughter was sitting on the bed.

"What's wrong, Red?" she asked.

"Your sister lied and told her dad that I was talking about sex on the phone and, basically, I have to leave." Tears were in my eyes by now.

Alana shook her head back and forth. It was as if she wasn't shocked or surprised.

"Now you see why I can't stand her. I wish I had a different little sister," she said.

"Don't say that. Regardless, that's ya blood. Don't be like me and my sisters," I told her.

Before she could respond, Aniya walked in. "Sis, don't think I'm putting you out. I just don't have the extra space."

It was like she knew that she was wrong because she kept trying to plead the fifth. I couldn't understand how she could just throw me out, when I did nothing wrong. I always stayed to myself because that's what I was used to. I didn't have friends back at home and I wasn't close to my siblings, so my go to place was my bedroom. I brought that same anti-social attitude with me to New York. I had nothing to say to Aniya, as she continuously tried to tell me she wasn't putting me out because I didn't want to cry. I had done enough of that and I refused to shed another tear.

51

Friend of Foe: The Beginning of the End of A Toxic Friendship

THE NEXT DAY WAS THE DAY I WENT TO THE SHELTER.

Aniya was supposed to come with me, but her cousin never came to take us. So, I explained to her that I was a big girl and that I could go by myself, even though the shelter was located in Brooklyn. I took the bus, then the train, and made my way to the shelter. Aniya kept in contact with me for a little while and, then, I told her I had to save my battery.

When I went in the building, it was two female security guards there. I was a bit nervous because I wasn't aware that a shelter had security.

"Hi, I was told to come here if I was homeless," I explained.

"Sign ya name and wait to be called. Curfew is at nine o'clock," the heavyset security guard told me.

"Can I leave after I check in?" I asked.

"Yea, just make sure you make it here by curfew," she told me.

I excused myself and went outside of the building to call Aniya.

"Hello? Sis, they saying I got a curfew and all."

"We'll just make sure you get back there on time, but just check in and come back here for now," she told me.

"Okay."

I hung up and went back inside. When I got in there, I checked in and they took all of my information. I didn't break down until I realized that I would be staying in a big room with fifteen other women, sleeping on cots. I knew I was homeless but, damn, did I have to live like it? I saw dirty needles in the bathroom, bloody tampons and shit in the toilets, and dirty panties. There was no way in hell I was going to be able to survive there, and all I could do was call Asia and break down.

"I can't do this Asia. I'ma go crazy in here. It's dirty in here, and these females on drugs in here. I know I'm homeless, but I don't want to live like this. I'd rather go back to Jersey," I cried.

"Where you gonna stay when you go back sis?" she asked.

"I don't know Asia, but I can't do this."

Asia didn't know what to say. She apologized time and time again because she truly thought that I would get a mini apartment until I got on my feet. She had no clue that I would be living in a shelter like that.

I didn't get to Aniya's house until later that day. I ended up spending almost all my money shopping and buying clothes that my fat ass couldn't fit, but I needed to do something to clear my mind. I made sure to save enough to get back to Jersey the next day. By the time I got back to Aniya's house, I didn't say much to her. I went to her daughter's rooms and just chilled with them until it was time to go to bed. I knew I had to get up in the morning to leave, so I made sure I got some rest. The next morning, I woke up and went to the avenue to buy a suitcase. When I got back, Aniya called me.

"What you doing sis?" she asked.

"I'm packing."

"Well, you not going back to Jersey. You gonna stay with my mother."

"Wow, are you serious?" I asked in complete shock.

"When I told you that you weren't going back to Jersey, I meant that."

I felt relieved. Aniya was making shit happen for me. She had kept her word, and I was grateful for that. So, that night, her cousin came to pick me up to take me to Far Rockaway. We had a great conversation on the way there, and it felt good to be around another one of her family members that was down to earth.

When I got to Sonya's house, Asia welcomed me in with open arms. She was so damn down to earth, and I just knew that we were going to get along.

"Sis, I'm so happy you here. We gon' have so much fun," Asia assured.

"Thanks, I'm just glad I don't have to go back to Jersey. I'm really tryna make it. I appreciate Aniya for talking to yawl mom, and I appreciate yawl mom for taking me in," I said.

"No problem sis, we got in, but why did you have to come here in the first place?" Asia asked.

"Because Aniya didn't have the extra room," I explained.

Asia rolled her eyes. "That's bullshit. She knew she didn't have the room before you moved here. Girl, you gon' see real quick why I don't fuck with my sister like that. She did the same shit to me when I was homeless. I love my sister to death, but she ain't right," Asia revealed.

I stood there with my mouth wide open. I didn't know what to believe or what to think. I didn't know if I should've believed Asia because my own sisters kicked my back in when I was doing nothing wrong, so I was skeptical because I didn't know if that was one of those situations.

52

Seeking Truth: Why Was I Hated?

I HAD FINALLY FELT LIKE I BELONGED. WHEN I FIRST moved in with Aniya's mother and sister, she treated me like I was one of her own. She took me to the welfare to help me get emergency food stamps, and Asia helped me sign up for housing. I woke up every day and went to my appointments, as well as my classes to get help with my place.

Things didn't start going downhill until my food was either being eaten or thrown in the trash. Whenever I said something, they would make up an excuse. I didn't feel like that was right, considering I bought my own food. When I reached out to Aniya and said something; she would tell me not to say anything and that I needed to put my name on my stuff, and I did just that and my belongings were still touched.

However, I didn't let that get the best of me. I still got up every morning and handled my business like a woman. I did what I had to do, and I was so proud of myself. I finally felt like an adult. I wasn't out doing young girl shit. I went out in the morning, handled my business, and came back home in the afternoon and played the game. I wasn't out fucking and sucking anyone or getting into trouble. I did the same thing every day, handled my business and played the game after. But, no matter how much I wasn't doing anything, no matter how anti-social I was, Aniya called me damn near every day saying one of her family members had an issue with me, and I just couldn't understand why. After a while, the stress started wearing on me.

Nobody cared until one day, Sonya's husband, John, introduced me to his nephew Wakeem. When I first met him, all he did was stare at me. I was looking a mess, so I figured that's why, and I didn't care. Hell, I wasn't used to guys wanting me anyway. It wasn't until the second time I met him that things really unraveled.

"Why you look so unhappy?" he asked.

I frowned my face up at him because I felt like he didn't know me to be questioning me or assuming anything, although he was right. I was very unhappy, but that was only our second-time meeting, so it bothered me for him to see that.

"What are you talking about? How you just gonna say I look unhappy?" I asked.

"I'ma street nigga. I can tell. I sensed it the first day I met you. Talk to me. You ain't gotta worry about it getting back to anyone. I don't fuck with this family like that. I come to see my uncle and that's it. They too judgmental for me," he explained.

He made me feel super comfortable, and I just went ahead and poured out everything I was feeling.

"I'm just so stressed. I never thought moving here would be like this. Every time I look, it's an issue with me. Whether it's my clothes, me leaving the house, or just my presence in general. I don't do anything for everyone to have a problem with me."

He wiped his hand down his face and leaned back on the couch. "It's jealousy. That's all it is. Ya best bet is to get ya shit together and get far away from these muthafucka's because it's gonna get worse, believe me."

I cocked my head back, like what the hell? It was one thing to be experiencing the fucked-up shit, but to hear someone that was their family tell me something like that was just crazy.

"What do you mean jealousy? Jealousy of what? I don't have shit?" I asked.

I remember being frustrated because it was like what the fuck could they be jealous of me for? I was struggling to survive day by day.

"Ya appearance, and the fact that you don't got shit but you still pushing forward. Some people can't handle another person's strength," he said.

I could understand what Wakeem was saying as far as the strength part, but everything else sounded crazy and unreal, and I wouldn't believe it.

"My appearance? I'm fat too! How the hell they gonna be jealous of me because of my appearance?!"

"You seen yaself? You're beautiful. Ya ass is fat, ya thighs is thick, and you got some nice ass titties. Ya whole shape is way better proportioned. I'm not just saying this because I'm attracted to you. I'm saying this because I know them. They don't want anyone coming around them that look decent or better than them. This family is weird. I bet you not even allowed to be alone in the house with my uncle, are you?"

At first, none of it made sense but, the more Wakeem talked, the more he made perfect sense. It was sad because I realized that the night I wore my boxer briefs, Aniya was eyeing me hard. It was a hateful look. It was a look like 'bitch, I really can't stand you'. That was a look she'd given me whenever I was in her presence, and I tried my best to shrug it off. I was from the projects, so I knew when a female wasn't feeling me, no matter what they said actions speak so much louder.

Needless to say, the next day, I was put out. So, everything Wakeem was saying made complete sense, only it was stupid to be jealous over something so stupid and small. However, I wasn't a married woman, so I couldn't speak from that behalf.

We talked more, and it seemed like we had talked his uncle up because that's who stormed in. He was completely confused and out of it.

"Unc, you okay?" he asked.

"Hey, Wakeem, I just need to talk to you for a second," John said.

Wakeem got up quickly. He was tripping over his shoes and everything. As they talked in the kitchen, I could hear crying. His uncle was crying, which had me extremely concerned. I thought he was hurt. I knew he was on drugs, and the first thing that came to mind was someone had hurt him. But, that assumption was quickly put to rest when Wakeem came back in the living room to sit down.

"Is he okay?" I asked.

"Yea, he good. He just need a hit."

I mouthed the word *wow*, because it was things like this that someone saw in movies or read in books.

"Honey, honey!" his uncle yelled. "Please help me pay this man! He's outside waiting for his money!"

I watched as Aniya's mother's husband stumbled through the tiny apartment screaming for his wife. I wasn't sure what happened then because the husband came and stood in the walk way of the living room just staring at us.

"Who is your friend?" he asked.

I laughed because I thought he was joking, but he really didn't remember who I was. I felt so bad for him.

"Unc, she lives here," Wakeem responded.

"Oh, hello young lady." John waved to me.

I waved back, and that's when his wife came and stood by him. I could see her hand something to him, and that's when he left out of the apartment.

"Um, Reds, you need to go to bed. You don't need to be out here with him," Sonya told me as she leaned on the chair that sat in the walk wat of the living room.

Wakeem looked at me and chuckled. I could tell he was shocked that I, a grown woman, was being told to go to bed. I really wanted to scream because I was twenty-three years old and here I was being told to go to bed.

I got up and went in the bedroom, just so there wouldn't be any tension, but I had already exchanged numbers with Wakeem, so we texted while I was in the bedroom.

Wakeem: You coming back out here?
Me: Yup.

I made sure Sonya was sleep before I went back out into the living room. He and I continued our conversation, and we even started watching YouTube on my phone. The next thing I knew, he was kissing me on my shoulder. I turned my head and my lips connected with his. He tongue-kissed me like my lips were the last lips he would be able to kiss.

I didn't stop it. I allowed him to lay between my legs on the couch. He lifted my shirt up and sucked on my titties. I stopped him because I didn't like my titties touched. He didn't ask any further questions. He stood me up and tongue-kissed me some more.

"I'ma put the condom on," he said.

"Nigga, what condom?" I asked.

This nigga had the nerve to pull a condom out his pocket.

"Oh, so you just planned on fucking me?" I asked.

"Yea. So, I came prepared, just in case," his response was honest.

I watched him pull his dick out, which wasn't small at all. The head of his dick was huge. I pulled my leggings down, and he turned me around and entered me from behind. I guess he was excited because he was doing me a little rough at first but, when I pushed him back, he whispered that he was going to go slow and that he did. I was soaked. Cum was dripping between my legs by now. It was a major stress reliever for me. We were fucking like no tomorrow until Asia came out the room. We jumped; I hurried and pulled my leggings up, and he pulled his sweats up. I sat on one couch while he sat on the other.

"Reds, you still up?" she asked.

"Yea, I'm about to go lay down now. We was just up talking."

Once I told her that, I got up and left out of the living room. I went into the bedroom I slept in and, before I could sit on the bed good, Wakeem was already texting me.

Wakeem: I want some more.

Me: Where we gonna do it at?

Wakeem: In the bathroom. Wait like ten minutes and then you go in first.

Me: Okay.

I was down with it because at this point, I didn't care. It wasn't that I was being spiteful. It was just that I was always targeted for doing nothing so, now,

I'ma do something. I waited the twenty minutes before heading in the bathroom. Once he heard the door close, seconds later, he got up and followed. I watched him put another condom on, and he turned out the lights, bent me over the sink, and slid his dick back inside me.

I bit my lip to keep from moaning because it felt so good but hurt at the same time because the head of his dick was so big. It was quiet in the bathroom, but we could hear the squishy sound every time he slid in and out of me.

Once he nutted, he tapped me on the ass and then turned the lights on. He flushed the condom down the toilet and then looked at me.

"I'ma leave out first. You stay in here for a few and then come out."

"Okay."

Once he left, I decided to wash up. I was allergic to latex and I knew I was going to be irritated the next day because I could already feel a slight irritation. When I was done washing up, I left out of the bathroom and went to lay down.

The next morning, I had an appointment, so I got up early, got myself together, and was getting ready to head out when the husband walked in. All I could do was shake my head because he had a completely different attitude.

"Good morning young lady." He smiled.

Just last night he didn't remember me, and now he did. I couldn't understand it but, since he was the only one who treated me with respect, I gave him the same in return.

"Good morning."

Asia walked into the kitchen furious. "Dad, I'm done. I'm tired of you and this lifestyle you living. I will take my kids and never come back!"

"Don't tell me what the hell to do. I'm your dad! I'm the adult. Don't tell me about how I'm living!" he yelled.

I stood back, watching everything go down. I knew it was about to get real when I saw Sonya coming down the hall.

"What's going on? Stop all that yelling in here."

"Shut the hell up! I pay the bills in here. I can yell if I want to!"

"Wait a minute now, don't tell me to shut up," she said.

"I'ma say what I want. She in here telling me about my lifestyle. If she wants to leave, then leave. I don't give a damn!"

He stormed out of the kitchen and went to the bedroom. When his wife followed, I went into the kitchen to see if Asia was okay.

"You good girl?" I asked.

"Hell yea. Ain't nobody worried about him. I'll beat his ass in here this morning," she responded.

I laughed and went on out to handle my business that day. That was something I did on a daily, I handled my business and, when I came back to the house, I played the game just to keep my sanity.

53

Friend or Foe: The Beginning of The End of A Toxic Friendship

I REMEMBER ONE DAY I WAS SITTING ON THE BED TRYING to get some typing down, when Aniya called me. I really didn't want to talk, but I picked up the phone anyway.

"Hello?"

"Hey, what you doing?" she asked.

"Sitting here tryna get some writing done."

"Oh, well, you know I gotta talk to you, right?" she asked.

I rolled my eyes because here she was coming to me with yet another problem that concerned me. It had begun to get so aggravating.

"What now?"

"Did you get smart with Asia's son? Because her baby dad called me saying how he don't like you and you better not say shit else to his kids or it's gonna be a problem."

I was super lost. For one, I didn't even know her kids' father and never been around him. For two, I never got smart with her kids, so all of this information was new to me.

"What? When was this?" I asked.

"I'm assuming it was the other night when yawl went to pick them up."

I did go with Asia to pick her kids up, but I never got smart with her son. I wasn't sure why I was being lied on but that was something I hated.

"So, if I got smart with his son, why didn't he say anything? Do you hear how you sound right now? That shit don't make no sense. If that's the case, then when he comes over here again, I'll say something to him to see if there's a problem."

"Oh, no, we not gon' do all that. I'm just telling you what was said," Aniya responded.

It was always a crime for me to speak my mind or even defend myself. This time was no different. Aniya was telling me that someone had an issue with me and, basically, I had to deal with it. I hated feeling backed into a corner. I hated feeling disrespected, and I hated feeling like I had to kiss ass just because I was in need.

"Why not? Look, I don't care if he from Brooklyn, Queens, or wherever. If there is an issue, it should be resolved."

"Hold on, this Asia right here."

"Hey, Asia, I supposedly got smart with your son? Because Aniya just told me that your baby dad called her saying how he don't like me and how I got smart with his fucking kids and it's gonna be a problem," I said.

"I never said that Reds. I said her baby dad called me and asked me who you were because he think you got smart with his son," she lied.

I had to look at the phone to make sure I was hearing right. This wasn't the first time that Aniya had lied and said she didn't say something. I couldn't understand her motive, but I knew it wasn't good.

"Aniya, you did say that. Why do I need to lie?" I asked.

"I was half sleep sis. I don't know what I said."

"Well, first of all, he never said any of that. He was basically asking me to ask you if you got smart with our son," Asia explained.

"Well, the way Aniya made it seem was like there was an issue and, if it was, I think we should wait until he comes by so we can talk about it and squash it."

"No, there ain't no issue, and we not gonna make it an issue. Those are his kids and he has every right to ask a question concerning his kids. He wanted to know if you got smart with his son and that's that."

Asia was coming off real defensive, and I didn't want any problems over miscommunication. I did notice how Aniya started a whole situation and then sat back being quiet because she didn't say one word while her sister was getting smart with me. I truly felt like Aniya wanted to cause problems between me and her sister.

When Asia got home that day, I had to pull her to the side and tell her how Aniya lied. I explained how I felt like, in a sense, Aniya might want us to fight because this wasn't the first time she'd lied about something.

So, that day when Asia came back home, I told her exactly what happened and how the situation was brought to me.

"I told you my sister was grimy, and she's a liar. I love her to death, but I don't fuck with her and now you see why. Reds, girl, I'm tellin' you, you better get on ya grind so that you can get ya place and be away from all this," Asia said to me.

It was so stressful hearing the words Asia spoke. I didn't know what to say in response or what to believe. One minute, Aniya was telling me this and that and, then, the next minute, Asia was telling me stuff as well.

"Why be grimy to me though?" I asked.

By now, Asia and I were in her room sitting on her bed.

"That's just who she is. Why you think I don't play her close? The only time I see her is at church or if I need my hair done and I ain't got the money to pay the shop. I don't fuck with her and she knows it," Asia said.

"I never knew yawl didn't get along like that. That's sad man, yawl just like me and my sisters."

"When Aniya didn't take me and my kids in when I was homeless, I knew that I had to leave her alone. She couldn't help me and my kids, but got a nigga that's not even family staying there? Girl, I stopped talking to her ass for months and I didn't regret it at all. It's just certain shit you don't do, and we all family and, regardless, we help each other. So, she showed me otherwise and I left her ass alone."

I could see how emotional Asia got while talking about the situation that led her and Aniya to stop talking at one point. She was hurt that her sister turned her away when she needed her the most, and it hurt me because I knew exactly what that felt like. I saw a lot of myself in Asia, and I think that's why we clicked the way that we did.

54

Friend of Foe: The Beginning of the End of A Toxic Friendship

I WAS THROUGH WITH LIVING IN NEW YORK BY NOW, and I was through with Aniya and her family, but I kept pushing because my goal was to change who I was before I left Jersey. However, Aniya just seemed so caught up on breaking me that we had yet another argument. We got into it when she called me while I was at the welfare office. I was having a good morning up until she called, and I had just gotten off the phone with my mother, so I was happy.

"Now, you know I gotta talk to you, right?"

I knew whenever she started it off like that, I was surely to be the topic of discussion. It never failed, there was always a problem with Reds.

"What's the problem now, and why am I on a conference call? Who on the other end?" I asked.

"Oh shit, girl, I just got off the phone with mommy. You know my ass don't know how to click over so the call will end," she said.

I knew she was lying but, at this point, I didn't care because she was the one who had something to prove, I didn't.

"Anyway, what you need to talk to me about?"

"What you do over auntie Pam house yesterday?" she asked.

"I was on the phone and then I went to sleep, why?"

"I thought you said you was going over there to type?" she questioned me.

I was already aggravated because she was always calling me with drama and, by now, I was frustrated because she was questioning me as if I wasn't grown.

"Um, I was, but my laptop was dead so while it was charging, I fell asleep. Any more questions? Like, what's the issue?"

"Hmm, well, Jay don't like you?"

"Okay, and? Am I supposed to be bothered because he doesn't like me?"

"Well, you know you my sis, and I gotta keep it real with you. I don't want you to be blindsided by anything or anyone," she said.

Aniya wouldn't have known what being real was about if it slapped her in the face. The entire time I lived in New York, she was spiteful, vindictive, and jealous for whatever reasons. It seemed as though she was helping me because I was staying with her family but, in all reality, she was hurting me and with no remorse.

"But, you're constantly coming at me with negative shit. It's never a dull moment with you. It's funny how everybody don't like me but, the moment I try to defend myself, it's a problem. So, what else you gotta talk to me about? You might as well get it all out now," I told her.

"It's not like that sis, but mommy keeps calling me about you not cleaning. Now, it's one thing for her to call me once, but every day she calls me and she said you done did something. Now, when my mother constantly has an issue, it becomes an issue for me."

I didn't like the way I was being talked to, nor did I like the way she was saying things. Like, bitch, if my mother got a problem with you, then I got a problem with you.

"This is crazy. Every day it's something and I don't be doing shit. I'm so tired of this shit. First, it was a problem with the way I was dressing; then, it was a problem with me always being in the room; then, it was a problem with the way that I talked and, now, it's some more bullshit. I'm so sick of this shit and, if ya cousin had such a problem, why didn't he come to me as a man? Since he so seven thirty crazy!"

Aniya always bragged about how her family was so crazy and how they all could fight. So, my thing was, if everyone was so crazy and about that life, then how come no one came to me personally? Why was it always behind my back? Why did they feel the need to indirectly bully me instead?

"Okay, now, I don't like how you talking to me right now-"

"I don't give a fuck. I'm tired of this. If I knew that I was going to go through all this bullshit, I would've kept my ass in Jersey. Matter of fact, I'll take my ass back to Jersey, since it's such a problem with Reds. I'd rather be homeless than to take anybody bullshit, especially when I know I don't be doing anything to anybody," I snapped.

I remember that day like it was yesterday, and I was beyond pissed. It made no sense that I had left Jersey just to move to New York for some more drama and bullshit, which wasn't my intentions at all. I was there to get on my feet and get my life together but, the longer I stayed, the more I went through.

"Alright," Aniya said.

I hung up on her because the conversation was done. I had nothing more to say and I didn't want to hear anything else she had to say. I hadn't even been called back yet to be seen, and I couldn't even focus anymore. I had to call my mom to let her know what happened because no matter what it was that was going on, I called her to let her know.

"Mom, don't you know Aniya just called me and told me how her cousin Jay don't like me and how her mom call her everyday complaining about me. Mom, I'm telling you now, I'ma snap the fuck out. They got me fucked up."

"Okay, Nunni, don't curse while you're on the phone with me; calm down and tell me what happened because I just got off the phone with Aniya and she saying that you cussed her out for no reason, and I told her that you don't go off without a reason."

"Mom, she's lying. She called me and told me that her cousin Jay didn't like me and how her mom keep calling her complaining about me. Mom, I don't be doing anything. All I do is go to my appointments, come back to the house and go in the room, or I'll play my game."

One thing about me, I wasn't a liar, and I made sure that I let my mother know everything that went on. I was there to change, so why would I just snap for no reason? That was two things I didn't like; don't lie to me and don't lie on me.

"Okay baby, calm down. Mommy don't want you getting into anything up there because I can't make it to you right away."

"Mom, I don't care. I'll fight all of them if I have to. I ain't no punk bitch and she keep coming at me like I'm one."

"Nunni, I get that, but mommy don't want you fighting down there. Don't let them make you come out of character. You're better than that," she said.

I tried my best to calm down, but it was hard. I hated to be picked on, and that's exactly what was happening. There was no excuse for how I was being treated. I couldn't even sit still anymore, so I walked out of the welfare office.

When I got back to the house, Sonya was mopping the floor. I was so angry and hurt, which was why I was already crying.

"Can I talk to yawl when yawl get a chance?" I asked them both.

"Yea, girl, I'll be in there," Asia said.

From the way she responded was as if she didn't know anything. I didn't care if she did or didn't. I was fed up and I was going to get my point across that day. While I sat and waited, my mother called me back.

"Is everything okay?" she asked.

"Yea, I'm back at the house now. I told Sonya and Asia that I needed to talk to them."

"Well, baby, when they get in there, try not to be so aggressive."

I'm not sure what came over me, but I broke down crying. "Don't tell me what to do. I'm not stupid, I know how to talk to people."

"Baby, I know you do, but I'm just saying humble yaself a little and don't be so aggressive."

"Mom, I'm tired. I don't do anything, and they just keep coming at me."

"I know baby, I know."

I could hear the hurt in my mother's voice. She wasn't near me and she didn't like violence or altercations, so the situation that was taking place bothered her. It bothered her to hear me hurting, and it bothered her that people constantly attacked me before getting to know me.

"I'll call you back. They bouta come in here soon," I told her as I wiped my face.

"Okay, remember, be humble. Mommy love you."

"I love you too."

As soon as they came in the room, I got straight to the point.

"Do yawl got a problem with me? Because I have no problem with leaving?" I said to them.

"Now, Reds, I don't have a problem with you living with me. You come in here with this attitude with us like we did something. All I want you to do is clean up after yourself."

"What don't I clean? Because I leave my sheet folded up on the bed? And I don't have an attitude, but I am tired of people having this mysterious problem with me."

"Yea, I just don't like anything on the bed," Sonya told me.

"Wait, and who got a problem with you?" Asia asked.

She was looking lost. Like, she really acted as if she didn't know what was going on. I didn't play her too close anymore because I was slowly but surely figuring out just how weird their family was.

"Supposedly, yawl cousin Jay got a problem with me. Saying how he don't like me, and I'm arrogant. Like me, out of all people, arrogant?"

"Reds, baby, that's not what was said. He said he wants to like you, but you come off as arrogant. I'm not sure where Aniya got her story from, but that's not how it was said," Asia explained.

"Well, that's how I got it and this not the first time Aniya done came to me telling me somebody got a problem with me. I mean, I'll leave. Because I'm tired of this. I left Jersey for a better life. I didn't come here to be in drama and, every time I look,

Aniya coming to me telling me yawl or somebody else in her family got an issue with me."

"Well, Reds, I ain't got no problem with you being here. I just ask that you don't keep nothing on the bed."

"Then tell me that. Don't go to Aniya acting like I'm such a problem because the way she keeps coming at me is negative and I don't like it at all. I told her I'll go back to Jersey if yawl don't want me here."

"Reds, it ain't no problem with you being here," Asia assured.

"Then, why don't nobody like me? I was going through hell and back with my family in Jersey. They didn't support me. It feels good to know that you're trying to be a big sister figure to me, Asia, and it feels good to be able to have a grandmother that cares about me. Well, at least I thought you did. I'm here trying to get on my feet and be a better person than I was."

I was in full blown tears. I was stressed, and I realized I had nowhere to turn. I didn't want to constantly stress my mother out because I knew the battle she was facing. I wanted change, and I wanted a better life. It just seemed like I was living in hell at this point.

"You and Aniya just need to sit down and have a talk because this is getting out of hand. Yawl both stubborn, and that's why yawl clash, but she also shouldn't be telling you lies about people not liking you because that's starting unwanted drama," Asia said.

"Nah, I don't want to talk. Because she's not going to listen. I barely talk to Aniya since I've been living with yawl. She just gives off this negative vibe and I don't want to be around that. When I went over her house last Sunday, the vibe was cold. Her husband didn't even speak to me, and why was that? I'm sure it's because she done told him some lies likes she always does. I don't want to be around that Asia."

I had finally let out my feelings. Well, some of them because it was much more where that came from. I remember watching Sonya leave the room. I wasn't sure if she couldn't take my emotional breakdown or if she had something to do.

***

Later that day, I remember sitting on Asia's bed when Aniya, her kids, and her cousin Marcus came in. It was unexpected, but I guess that was another one of her infamous pop-ups. I didn't speak to anyone because I didn't care to. Her oldest daughter spoke to me, and that's when I spoke back.

"Ya ass like to hang up on people," Aniya laughed.

"I didn't hang up on you. The conversation was done," I responded.

I wasn't quite sure how I ended up in the living room, but I remember sitting on the floor playing my game while Aniya and Marcus went to the store.

"Oh, Reds, my mother gonna beat you up?" Devin said to me.

"Um, beat who up? Ain't nobody touching me."

"Dang, shut up. You always running ya mouth," LaLa snapped at Devin.

This was the second time Aniya came to her mother's house in sneakers, jeans, and a scarf on. I really felt like she was trying me. Like, she wanted to fight but bullying me was her way of doing so. I tried to brush it off by continuing to play my game. I knew for a fact that Aniya kicked my back in to her family. It was no secret because they showed it just by the way they acted towards me or by certain things they said.

"Say what you gotta say. Because I'm getting phone calls of how you kicking my back in. This is my family so whatever you say to them about me, they gonna tell me," she said.

Aniya and her cousin was back from the store now. She had come in the living room and she sat on the couch with her legs open like a guy would. Now, here I was trying to figure out when and where I said anything negative about her or when I kicked her back in. I expressed my feelings to Asia and Sonya as to why I didn't deal with Aniya. I didn't think I said anything wrong, but it is what it is. Now, it made me wonder who really told her what, and it had to be between her mom or sister.

"I didn't say anything bad. I just said how our relationship wasn't the same since I moved here, and how I really don't care to talk to you anymore like I used to."

"So, what's this about me being negative? How am I negative? I'm always trying to help you. I made sure you didn't go back to Jersey. I moved you in my mother's house. I brung you around my family? So, how am I being negative?"

I wanted the conversation to be done because now, I felt like she was throwing stuff in my face. If you're going to help someone, then help them, but don't get upset and throw it in their face for some sort of confirmation.

"That's all nice, but I feel like you're negative. Whenever you call me, it's either about something someone said about me. Someone not liking me or an issue you got with me. That's what I mean by negative," I explained.

"Reds, I be tryna have your back. I don't want you being blindsided at all. I don't come at you negative. I'm just trying to help you. That's all I've been doing is trying to help you. Your attitude is gonna stop you from going places. This is why I can't introduce you to the people I'm working with. I'm doing a lot for you behind the scenes, and I don't say anything because you always think someone is trying to hurt you or you have an attitude."

"What attitude? Yawl keep saying I have this attitude when I don't and, at this point, I don't even care anymore."

"You do have an attitude. I never let a female disrespect me the way you did earlier. My own sister never came at me the way you did, and that's my blood."

"Well, I'm not apologizing because I don't feel like I disrespected you and, if anything, I feel disrespected because this is the second time you pulled up like you wanted to fight."

"Reds, I will never fight you. Me and my sister argue like cats and dogs and it never led to fighting. I brought you down here to help you, not hurt you. I keep telling you that I don't bring any and everyone around my family. We all welcomed you in with open arms, and I don't know what else to do to show you that," she explained.

I figured out a long time ago that Aniya was the type of person that never would own up to her wrongs, so us having that discussion was pointless. She was always going to feel like she was right, and I was wrong. That wasn't the first time I realized how shady Aniya was, and I just couldn't find myself eating with someone who bragged about feeding me.

Once Aniya finally left, Asia came to me while I was in the bedroom getting my clothes out to shower.

"So, how did yawl talk go?" she asked.

"Basically, she said how she only tells me stuff to have my back and how whatever I say to yawl that yawl tell her."

"Yawl who? Girl, I don't talk to her like that. She's lying, but you see she ain't say that shit while I was sitting in there because she knew that I would call her out," Asia said.

I shrugged my shoulders. Everything and everybody was confusing. I was tired of all the drama, and it basically surrounded me. Aniya had it out like I was such a big burden and such a big problem to her family. I didn't come to New York for that. I came to get my shit together and change.

55

Seeking Truth: Why Was I Hatred?

Shit was getting too hectic in New York. It went from being positive to negative, and I had come too far to relapse and go back to the person I was. I finally realized it was time for me to go when the night before it was my time to visit my mother, I updated a status on Facebook saying: No matter how old you are, misery loves company.

I had just gotten off the phone with my mother when she was telling me about how my sister Linette had been giving her problems and doing everything in her power to see her unhappy, which was my reasoning of updating the status.

At that time, Sonya came into the living room and looked me up and down.

"You need to pull your shirt up," she said.

I never took my eyes off the TV, but I did pull my shirt up, which was already up at the time. Sonya then left out of the living room and, about five minutes or so later, she came in the living room and sat down.

"Reds, I don't be tryna be smart, but I have a husband and it's about respect. I can't have you walking around here in spaghetti strapped shirts around my husband."

"I heard you the first time. This is your house, and you don't need to explain anything to anyone you're allowing to stay here twice," I responded.

Sonya didn't say anything. All she did was get up and leave out of the living room. I don't know what transpired that night but, the next day, Asia came to me while I was packing up my PS3 because my ride was going to be there soon.

"Girl, what happened last night?" Asia asked.

"Huh? What are you talking about?"

"Girl, Aniya called mommy and told her you was kicking her back in on Facebook. Something about her being miserable and what not. They told me, and I said I'll talk to you to see exactly what happened," Asia explained.

I could feel my body heating up, and I could feel myself wanting to say some real raunchy things, but I kept my composure because I truly felt like they wanted me to come out of character, and I just wasn't about to do that since I had changed so much.

"That's some real foul shit. Why would I talk about yawl mom when she gave me a place to stay? This shit is getting out of hand now. I'm so tired of Aniya and her damn lies."

"I feel you, girl. I read the status and I didn't think it was about mommy, but Aniya called her and told her that you was talking about her."

"So, if that was the case, then why she ain't pull up like she normally do? Why you ain't come drag me if I was talking about yawl mom? Come on now Asia, that doesn't make any sense. I'm so tired of this shit. I'm so glad I'm leaving for a couple of days because this shit is so petty, and Aniya is a sneaky ass bitch."

"Sis, you right. This is petty, and I'm so over the drama and I can tell that you are too. I'm glad you getting away for a little. I can see the stress all in ya face and it don't make no sense how you're being treated. I don't know why Aniya would bring you here just to do all this, and it's sad, but I need you to know one thing. If you get home and don't want to come back, then don't come back. You ain't gotta come back nowhere that you're miserable at and know that I'ma always be here for you. But, just to clear the air, go in there and let mommy know that you wasn't talking about her because regardless if they be there for you, just know I'll always be there for you."

I genuinely thought Asia was a true friend. I took her words to the heart because she showed me more loyalty than her sister did. So, I went to get dressed, packed my bags, and then I went into Sonya's room.

"Hey, Aniya called you and told you that I was talking about you on Facebook?" I asked.

She nodded her head yes.

"That's so ignorant and malicious on her end but, just so you know, I wasn't talking about you. I would never do that and, if that was the case, why didn't anyone say anything to me if they felt like it was about you?" I asked.

"I don't know Red, but like I said last night. I have a husband. I don't have no problem with you being here, but the way you dress is inappropriate at times and I can't have that around my husband. Just like when I go down south to visit my sister. I'ma make sure I wear stuff to cover me up because everyone down there is married," she explained.

"I get that, and cool. I just wanted to apologize if you felt a way about what was told to you because this is your house."

Those were my last words before my male friend knocked on the door. I went to open it, and he helped me with my bags. I took the majority of my things because I did plan to come back. My friend and I got outside of the complex and we saw John.

"Hey, young lady, are you leaving?" he asked.

"Yes, I have to. Your wife said the house will be empty because yawl all going down south."

John shook his head, and he looked disappointed.

"Young lady, I wasn't invited. I'll be here while they're on vacation."

My face was frowned up by now because the entire time, all Sonya kept saying was that I had to leave because they were all going down south for a couple of weeks, and she didn't want to leave me in her house alone.

"Are you serious? Why would she tell me to leave then? I could have continued to go to my classes so that I could still get paid," I asked him.

"Honey, that's just my wife. This ain't the first time she lied and it won't be the last. I just deal with it."

I walked away without saying anything. It was no secret that I was treated like shit while staying with Sonya, but to know that she would lie just to get me out of her house was sad and low down.

On my way home, I called and told my mother how Aniya had lied and told Sonya that I was talking about her on Facebook, and I also told her what John had said as well. During my ride to Jersey, which was a total of four hours because we stopped for food, I noticed that Aniya had been throwing major shots on Facebook. I noticed it, readers noticed it, and my mother noticed it as well. I was so over her and her Facebook gangster ass and so was my sister Linette because she made a status in my *Kickin' It With Reds* readers group and let it be known that me and her may not get a long, but she'd fuck any bitch up over her baby sister.

Of course, Aniya saw it and updated a status, which I didn't see, but my mother called me and told me about it.

"Don't worry about it baby because I went in her inbox and asked her who she was talking about and she said somebody she use to work wit. I know she lying, but don't worry about it baby; continue to play ya game," she said.

My mother thought I was still in New York. I didn't tell her that I was coming down early because in all reality, I was supposed to leave that Friday instead of that Wednesday, but I wanted to surprise her, and that I did.

56

Trying To Rebuild: Game Plan

WHEN I GOT BACK TO JERSEY, I WAS FINALLY ABLE TO complete my Harmony and Chaos series. No, it still didn't do well, and I didn't make but three hundred dollars off my entire series. I realized that I needed to take yet another stand. I contacted Tommy and let him know that I thought it would be best if he released me and my series, so I could see how it did under the name Reds Johnson.

He complained that he would be losing out on money, and how he's sorry that things didn't work out, but he would release me and my books. That same night, the Harmony and Chaos series had been taken down. I did feel a little bad because Tommy had signed me when no one else would. But, I had to take emotions out of it. My books were my babies, and I did what was best for me and my babies at that time.

***

During the rereleasing of my books, Aniya contacted me. The shit she said was so slick and that was the second time I had lashed out at her because I was tired of her coming at me sideways, like I was supposed to bitch up because she was from New York.

"Yo, we gonna fight," she said.

"Um, what?" I responded.

"What did I tell you about having an issue with me and not coming to me about it? I don't know how many times I tell you that whatever you got to my family about, it's going to get back to me regardless."

"Um, what the hell is you talking about? What issue?"

"Asia said that you must've still been mad at me for telling mommy that you was talking about her on Facebook. I told her that I didn't know what she was talking about."

"I wasn't mad, but I did say what you did was real fucked up for telling ya mom that I was talking about her on Facebook. I sure the fuck did say you was foul as fuck for that. But mad? I been over that. I left that in New York the day I left," I said.

"Wooooow. I never called Asia. Mommy called me and was like I don't think Red likes me, and I said why. She said that she told you to pull ya shirt up and you got smart with her. I was like mom, really? Reds got smart? Why would she get smart knowing that you're my mother?"

"See, that's the bullshit and that's why I'm glad I left. Yawl got too much shit going on with yawl. Asia lying and ya mom lying. I can't take this shit and it's sad because yawl grown women. Ain't nobody get smart with ya mom. Like, why would I do that when I'm staying with her?" I asked.

"Exactly, that's what I was thinking like, why would she get smart with my mom. I just kept telling them like Reds is my friend; she wouldn't do that to my mom knowing how I feel about her."

For some reason, I felt like Aniya was lowkey trying to threaten me. She kept stressing the fact that she didn't think I would get smart with her mom because it was her mom.

My attitude was on one thousand by now because the way she came off was so cocky. It was like 'bitch I'm going to put fear in your heart and that's that'. Of course, over the years, Aniya had said a lot of slick shit out of her mouth and claimed she meant no wrong, and I let it slide but, after a while, I was like fuck that shit. I shed blood on my own sisters, so what the fuck made her so different?

57

Friend or Foe: The Beginning of the End of A Toxic Friendship

DURING MY TIME BACK IN JERSEY. I MANAGED TO GET signed to Mrs. Clark. I was so ecstatic because I had been trying to get signed to her since I was fourteen years old. I was so scared to announce that she signed me, so my mother announced it and then Linette announced it.

"Nunni, you deserve this. It's your time to shine, so shine on baby girl."

Finally, I announced it, and I got a lot of support but also a lot of backlash. People were saying how stupid she was for signing me and how I didn't deserve to be signed to someone that good because my work wasn't that good. They took a moment that I had fought for, for years, and turned it into a bashing moment.

Aniya even called me and, instead of her being supportive, it kind of felt like she wasn't happy either.

"Why I gotta go to Facebook to see that you done got signed to Mrs. Clark? Like, how the fuck did that happen? How did you get her to sign you, and why wasn't I the first one to know about it?" she asked.

I didn't know how to take what she said, but I didn't let it kill my moment because Facebook had already done that. I just knew that I had to step away from her in order to keep my focus.

On top of me having to fulfill my contract, I was back helping my mother, while my sister Linette constantly gave men her hard-earned money. Thankfully, I was still getting food stamps from New York, and the little bit of royalties I received from my books were helping out just enough. But it seemed like the more I tried to bounce back, the more trials stepped in my way. I was trying to rerelease my books, and I needed help doing so.

I contacted Mitchell, who had been my graphic designer when I was signed to Praise & Glory Publications. I knew that the money I was receiving from my royalty checks wasn't enough to get covers done so I could get my books back up, so I hit him up and asked him for help. He agreed, and he helped me as much as he could. My mother was using her child support checks, which was only one hundred and forty dollars every week to help me pay for the covers I was getting done.

She paid Mitchell fifty dollars every week and, sometimes, she missed a payment and had to double up, considering sometimes she didn't get paid the child support. Everything was good until she missed a few payments and, although money talks, both myself and my mother explained that he would get paid in full once we got the funding and to just be a little patient with us if he could.

Instead of Mitchell responding to either one of us, he ignored us. I told him to just forget it and I'd find someone else to help me. It hurt because I really needed the help, but I just didn't have the money. I was sleeping on a roach infested couch at my sister Linette's house. I was trying my best to help my mother keep food in the fridge because my sister kept giving up her paycheck to the guy she was dealing with. And I was just trying to remain strong and keep writing, but it was hard when I didn't have shit.

I'm guessing Mitchell finally decided to respond because he sent me a long message on Facebook.

Mitchell: *What's up Reds. This conversation is late, but it needs to happen. You got mad because you felt like I was just ignoring you. The last question you asked me threw me because you asked me how much for the covers, but you were having problems with the other payments, which was understandable. But what had me dumbfounded is how are you going to pay for the four covers, but you could not make your scheduled payments on the payment schedule you set up? So, I had no answer.*

As long as I have been dealing with you, I look at you like a little sister, a bratty one, but when it all boils down to it, I was going to get you straight, but I have a million things going on. I'm trying to get my paper too. But you were not getting pushed to the back or forgotten.

Reds: Hey, and the arrangement was two hundred a month. But, after discussing with my mother and looking at the western union receipts, we realized we paid for all the covers that I received. I thought I was back in payments but, as I looked at it, I felt like I wasn't because I wasn't getting anymore covers. I came to you and asked for those four eBook covers because I actually had a way to pay for them at the time.

You could have said something, anything, but I was ignored a few times and I felt that wasn't right. I had been talking to Aniya and seeing her post new covers, so I just didn't understand why I wasn't getting the same treatment as her. But, I understand you have a lot going on. Which is why I said you could have told me and I would have been patient.

Mitchell: *I feel you, but I did just step into a new position and I had to straighten up that situation. I was actually just going to surprise you with the covers whether you made the payments or not, but that shit did not happen. I think we both felt insulted, so we need to have some better communication both ways.*

Reds: *I'm not sure if you felt insulted by the payments not being made on time, but it wasn't like I just wasn't going to pay. I was and still am in a messed-up situation, but I have very few people that believe in me and rock with me so, if someone is helping me, I wouldn't dare fuck them over. I just truly felt disrespected and I felt as if you didn't take or look at my career as important.*

Mitchell: *I know what your situation is and, no, you did not insult me by not making payments on time. My brain does not click right sometimes, and I usually end up making a mess. I read the situation wrong and, instead of getting pissed, I had to let the situation breathe.*

Of course, I want to see you shine, you are part of the fam. So, when I come your way, I want shit to be right, not rushed. I watch all of your releases; your new book is Harmony and Chaos 2 *and you will be releasing your story soon.*

Reds: *Well, I appreciate you coming to me and the kind words. I appreciate the love* *and support and you wanting to see me shine. I do tend to get in my feelings when I feel disrespected, but you're right as far as our communication needing to be better. Hopefully, we can move past this*

Mitchell: *I stopped getting mad at you years ago. Just waiting so we can get back to work.*

That was the end of the first feud Mitchell and I had. I was appreciative of everything he'd done for me. It was because of him, Terry, and another author that I was able to get my books back up. However, there had been times that Aniya had come to me and told me that Mitchell wasn't saying nice things about me when it came to paying him for covers I got done but, then, in the same token, she would say how he wanted to help me. I was more than confused because I thought Mitchell and I had a good friendship, but he quickly let me know that he valued Aniya and her career more.

Reds: *Hey Mitchell! How are you? Is there any way you can make a banner or promo with a picture of me and all of my books?*

It was getting harder for me to promote all of my books separately, so I thought by getting one big banner made with all of my books on it would save me time. Considering Mitchell was the one that was helping me and he told me whenever I needed him he would be there, I decided to go to him. He didn't respond until a day or so later.

Mitchell: *Hey Reds, I'm not ignoring you, just thinking about it.*

Reds: *Okayy Mitchell! No problem.*

Mitchell took his time responding to me, and that was cool. I knew he had a lot on his plate and that he was doing me a major favor, so I was patient through the entire ordeal. But, when he finally reached back out, it was tension.

Mitchell: *Can't do it. I'm trying to get this money so, if it's not about money, it's not about me.*

Reds: *Wait, huh? Is this responding to what I asked?*

Mitchell: *Yeah, the ad, can't do it. I agreed to help you with some covers, so I gotta keep it like that. It's nothing personal* *and I know you are fucked up right now, but I am too so something has to give.*

Reds: *Okayy, well you most certainly didn't have to come off that way. I appreciate all that you've done, and not once have I ever tried to use you or take advantage. No, the payments aren't constant, and I understand you need your money and nothing is for free. But, there is a way to go about things. I'm sure you never came at Aniya like this, but it's cool. I'll find someone else to do it. God bless.*

Mitchell: *Aniya is a totally different person. Many blessings to you as well.*

The way Mitchell came at me was wrong, in my opinion. It was also very confusing because one minute he wanted to help me and, then, the next minute, he wasn't fucking with me, so it made me feel like someone was in his ear about something. I brought up Aniya because she was always calling me and telling me how much he was doing for her and she didn't have to pay him for anything.

Granted, we were two different people, but we were both taken advantage of in the industry and we were both struggling trying to bounce back. Why treat me fucked up? Why act as if my career didn't matter or act like I didn't deserve your help? I didn't respond to Mitchell then, and I didn't respond to him when he came back in my inbox.

Mitchell: *I just finished reading over my message again. I guess it could be misconstrued, but I did not say anything out of the way to you, besides the fact that I did not want to do your ad. I also went as far as to say that it was not personal. I did not ask you for any money because that is not a conversation we need to have. All of that extra stuff you did bringing other people into our conversation was not unexpected. But, if we are only cool when I do what you want, then we are not that cool huh?*

It wasn't about doing what I wanted. It was about him keeping his word. I had so many people turn their backs on me, and for him to say he'd always be there and then flip was confusing. I sent my mother the screenshot of how he came off, and I sent Aniya a screenshot.

Aniya: *Why do yawl keep bringing me up?*

Reds: *I brought you up because for some reason, he keeps comparing us, as if you're better than me. I'm not allowing anyone to come at me like that.*

Aniya: *I done cussed Mitchell out a few times for bringing me in yawl mess. He really needs to stop.*

Those were her words to me, but I knew that other things were said when she had conversations with Mitchell. There was no way he would just flip on me the way that he did without something being told to him. I had seen it one too many times during my time in the industry and, soon after that, Mitchell deleted me off Facebook. So, how much did he really support me?

58

Skeptical: Why Did She Care About Me So Much?

DURING MY HARDSHIPS, I ALSO HAD ANOTHER WOMAN I called my friend and my sister. Nichole, who was also an author. She had been supporting me and riding with me since day one and it was weird as ever, but she was a true friend. When I needed money, food, or help, she was there. When I needed a shoulder to cry on, she was there, and I couldn't understand why. Everyone else had turned their backs on me and did me wrong, so why was she still there?

Nicki: Reds did u change your name on fb luv? I was about to tag u and I can't find u?

Reds: No, I didn't. I deactivated my page. Going through some things.

Nicki: Oh ok. I'm sorry luv. I've been there. I was just wondering. Are you ok tho?

I'm Here anytime... I'm just sayings. Please stay in touch. I'm just concerned because Trina is no longer on fb and she just hit me up Saturday and then she is off fb. So, I'm like where is my team? 😫

Reds: It's okay and thank you. I appreciate it. I really do, but I'm not big on sharing my problems with people. I'll be back soon. I just need to get my thoughts together.

Nicki: I understand, and I wasn't trying to get in your business. I was genuinely concerned boo. Stay up and take it easy. 💕💚

Reds: Thank you again love 💚

Nicki: You're welcome boo!

I didn't see it back then, but I realized it soon after that she was really concerned for me. She took me under her wing and played that real big sister role. She was there when I was homeless, and she was there through the ups and downs with Aniya. She always gave me encouraging words and, whenever I wanted to quit writing, she would tell me not to. She had given me money when I was without, and she had stopped me from committing suicide a few times.

Whenever I thought less of myself, she was the one putting me on a pedestal. When I talked bad about myself, she spoke good about me; when I didn't think I was good enough, she was telling me how I was good enough and more. I even stopped talking to her because she was still signed to BTBP, but I realized she had to move accordingly and, even then, she was still supporting me and still being there for me when I didn't deserve it and, still to this day, she is there for me. I can actually call her my big sister without regretting it. I can actually call her my friend and mean it, and it feels damn good to have someone genuinely in my corner besides my mother.

59

Internet Dating

I HAD KNOWN ISAIAH FOR SEVERAL MONTHS NOW, AND he was another guy I had met off the internet. POF, to be exact and, when we first met, we spent hours on the phone. He was sexy ass hell, body was crazy and tatted, and he had a nice car with a good job. It felt good to come across a guy like him.

We finally met in person, and we ended up fucking in his car because I couldn't bring him in my sister's house due to me sleeping on the couch and the house being infested with roaches. I had no intentions on sleeping with Isaiah, but he said we had to have sex if I wanted to continue to deal with him because he loved sex.

We fucked and, after that, he was acting funny. I always blamed myself for when stuff like that happened. So, I wondered was my sex bad? Did I stink? Those were always the main questions. But, that wasn't it, and I found out a week or so later that it was more than that. I went to the doctors and found out that I had Chlamydia and, when I reached out to Isaiah to tell him what I found out, he blocked me. He blocked my number from his phone and blocked me from Snapchat. I broke down crying to my mother because I couldn't understand how someone could do that.

"He knew he had something and, once you found out and confronted him, he didn't like that. Don't worry about him blocking you. Be thankful that you have something that's curable; let karma take care of him," she said.

60

Living Life or At Least Trying To

I MET TC JUST A COUPLE OF MONTHS AFTER I HAD LEFT New York. He hit me up on POF and, once I saw that he was from Millville, New Jersey, I was like nah. I was cautious when it came to dealing with any guy from around my way. Not only because I was raped, but because everybody knew everybody.

I hit my home girl Porsha up and asked her about him. She knew everybody and they mama, so she was my go to person when I wanted the scoop on someone.

"Girl, that's my homeboy Timothy. They call him TC tho'. He a good dude, but he hustle. He take care of his kids too. Oh, and he about that life so don't think you gonna be talking crazy to him," she explained to me.

I had mad love for Porsha. She was Jimmy's ex-girlfriend, and she was the only person who truly wanted to know the reason behind me always staying in my room.

"Can I ask you somethin'?" she asked.

"Yea, wassup?"

"Why you always in ya room? Don't that get boring?"

It was weird that she had asked me such a question because no one cared enough about me to find out. There had been times where my father would come in my room wondering if I was finally dead or not because they hadn't seen me in days.

"I just do."

I didn't really care to go into detail because I felt like she was just like everyone else. Someone who acted like they cared but really didn't. But, she was different because once she found out that I didn't have any friends and that I was afraid to go out because I was raped, she made sure she changed all that.

"I got you. It's time for you to start living life. I been through some things similar to you, and living my life has helped me get over a lot," she told me.

Porsha had me just like she said because she was the reason why I experienced a lot. She took me to my first bar when I was twenty-one. She took me to my first club, and she took me to my first college party. Life was lit when it came to going out with Porsha but, just as much as she did for me, I did for her. I had given Porsha a total of four hundred dollars because she said she needed some extra cash.

After that, Porsha started treating me differently, always declining me when I wanted to go out with her. Always saying that if I didn't have money, then I couldn't go or making some excuse that her car was full. The shit hurt my feelings, and my brother walked up on one of the conversations I was having with my mother about her.

"I told you I didn't want you being friends with her, and this is why. Because she's fake. I wasn't being mean when I said that," he told me.

I thought that Jimmy was being mean but, all along, he was right. Porsha had done me so wrong time and time again. Her friends did me wrong time and time again and, when it came to us being around men, I was the one that never got any play because I was the dark-skinned fat girl of the crew.

***

I ended up messing with TC and, soon after that, he got locked up. Me being the type of female I was, I reached out to him, and he reached back out telling me he need money to help him until he got out. I sent him what I could and asked could I visit him. When I did, I got no response back. I thought maybe he was on lockdown and that he couldn't receive or send letters but, when I called the jail, they had told me that he had been released already.

The shit fucked my head up like damn, you took my money and couldn't respond to let me know when you was getting out? You couldn't even hit my phone up to let me know that you was out? I couldn't understand why I kept running into dudes like that. But, even though I felt stupid and what he did was wrong, I still found some way to get him to respond to my text so that we could meet up and I could give him his birthday present that I had gotten him while he was locked up, considering he'd got locked up on his birthday.

61

Catching Feelings Too Fast

I MET MIKE AROUND SEPTEMBER BECAUSE TC GOT locked up around that same time. So, in the midst of me waiting for him, although we weren't together, I came across another guy. Mike hit me up on POF, and I thought he was a girl at first. He had the prettiest face. Once I found out he was a guy, we exchanged numbers. He would text me every day, but I would respond late due to me being so tired from stress or writing. Of course, I never told him that I was stressing, but he did know I worked. I told him I worked at Wal-Mart, the same thing I told most guys after I realized they would use me or try to use me once they found out I was an author.

Mike was a sweetheart and, when we finally met for the first time, I was happy. He had traveled about forty minutes just to see me, and that felt so good to me. The fact that he didn't mind coming to see me meant everything and he didn't even know it.

"Wassup girl?" he greeted me when I got in his car. He gave me the warmest hug, and his vibe was so chill and down to earth.

I had caught feelings for Mike when I shouldn't have, but he was nice to me; something I had never experienced from a guy. He didn't mind being seen with me, and he didn't mind paying for me whenever we went out.

62

Catching Feelings Too Fast

IT WAS THE END OF 2017, AND MY BIRTHDAY WAS JUST A few days away. Mike was supposed to help me celebrate my birthday. I was so excited because for one, I had never spent my birthday with a guy before and, for two, it felt good to actually have plans for my birthday.

However, the day of my birthday, Mike shitted on me.

"So, we're not hanging out?" I asked.

"Girl, no. You don't need me to hang out with you. It's ya birthday, so you do what you want," he responded.

I broke down crying in the passenger seat of Shanda's car. When she got in, all she could do was start the car and shake her head.

"Don't cry Nunni, don't cry."

I had never forgiven Mike, but that didn't stop me from hanging out with him and continuously having sex with him unprotected. I had fallen for Mike because I knew he was a good person, but he had been done wrong in his past, which resulted in him not wanting to get close to any female, well at least not me.

He had lost his mother, and I knew once a man lost his mother that he wouldn't have any trust, love, or respect for women because the only woman they truly cared about was gone. I wanted to be there for Mike, even after he had hurt me time and time again. I wanted to show him that I genuinely cared about him, and it wasn't because he had a nice car or that he had a nice house; he was cute and had great sex.

I genuinely wanted to be there for him. I wanted to be that someone he could call on just to vent to when he felt like he was about to explode. Mike held a lot in and, considering I had a lot of my mother in me, I was kind of good at reading people when I wanted. I knew he didn't let out how he truly felt, and I wanted to be that person to let him know that it was okay to do so.

I even went as far as to buying his son Christmas presents, and what hurt me the most was when he said fuck them by his actions because he had never come to pick up the presents. It showed me that he didn't care, yet, for some reason, I continuously fought to show him that I was different.

However, no matter how much I fought, Mike continued to push me away. He continued to hurt my feelings and bluntly let me know that he wasn't feeling me the way that I was feeling him, and he couldn't see himself in a relationship with me.

But, even then, I still was trying. At this time, Mike's birthday was coming up and I wanted to do something special for him. I wanted to show him some appreciation, considering he always paid for our dates whenever we went out. So, my plans were to rent a room, have balloons set up everywhere, a cake, wine, and rose petals. I was going to have his birthday card lying on the bed with money inside.

My plans were to give him two hundred dollars towards his California trip or his car to get fixed. It wasn't much, but I just wanted to show him that I really cared about him and that I had his back through anything.

But, when I contacted him about the dates so that I could book the room, he declined me, which was nothing new. Whenever I wanted to spend time with Mike, he declined me or made up some excuse as to why. I was so upset because I had just found out that he was dealing with a girl from around my way, and I was not one to judge but she looked like a man.

I found this out by going on his Instagram and seeing him and the girl talking. As women, we know when a guy done fucked a girl, is dealing with a girl or have dealt with a girl; it's just our intuition. They both made it obvious that they were dealing because he would leave comments like hey beautiful, damn you sexy, or I miss you. Then, in return, she would say things like you're so cute, text me, or what you doing with heart eyes under his pictures. Yeah, it was simple, but the simple things had meanings behind them.

What hurt me the most was when I found out that he had spent time with her on her birthday, which was in November, but dissed me for my birthday, which was in December. I remember his exact words: "Don't be dry bday girl. We gonna turn up ASAP!"

There were numerous times that I wanted to chill with Mike, and he turned me down just like all the other guys. He complained about how far I was, yet he was dealing with another female from around my way, so what was really the problem? He went from showing that he liked me to not liking me at all. Every time we talked, we argued, and it showed how disgusted with me he truly was. I didn't know what it was that I did, and I was tired of it.

There were over one hundred text messages between me and him going back and forth, but what stood out to me the most and hurt me the most was the last couple of text messages we exchanged.

Me: *You can eat my ass and pussy on a bloody day. How's that? Since you just keep texting me but I'm so irrelevant in your life. Mike, I'll violate you and the little bit of family you got left and beat up ya bitches. I don't understand how a nigga that can't stand me, don't wanna be around me, always tryna hurt me still talking? K.*

Mike: *Ok now u bringin' my family in??? wrong move desperate fuck. I'll invade ya whole shit bitch wit no emotions afterwards,* *fuck u and them gifts. I'll make u eat them gifts u fat bitch. action speak louder than words. I'm done talk'n. Spend that shit.*

Me: *Now I'm a fat bitch? Can you say something else? Like we established the fat part. & yea, you really slow. I said I'll violate the little bit of family you got left. NEVER said NOTHING about ya family. You so pressed. But yet you fucked my fat ass numerous times. Mike, like I said before. You not bout it.*

That was the last time I spoke to Mike or heard from him. I couldn't front and say that I wasn't hurt that he disrespected me the way that he did, but I had said my wrong as well. My lashing out was out of hurt because I knew that he was spending time with other girls, and I felt like he only dealt with me when it was convenient. I didn't understand why I wasn't pretty enough to him. Why he couldn't spend time with me? Why he couldn't see more in me than what he did?

Him saying fuck me and the gifts hurt as well. He had showed me time and time again that's how he really felt, but for him to actually say it hurt me more. It was because of him that I decided to title my memoir *Fat Bitch*. I had been so tired of being called that and being hurt by it that I decided to embrace the pain and turn the negative into a positive.

63

Friend or Foe: The Beginning of The End of A Toxic Friendship

ANIYA WAS STILL BEING SHADY, AND IT SEEMED TO HAVE gotten a bit worse. Whenever I would update a status, there she was updating statuses to prove whatever imaginary point she had. I was trying my best to push past the bullshit, but I just couldn't. There had been many nights I cried to my mother about how bad Aniya hurt me and how I just couldn't be her friend anymore. I had three blood sisters that shitted on me, and I had befriended females in the industry that shitted on me. I truly thought Aniya was not only my friend but my sister, and she hurt me. I mean, she hurt me bad.

"Baby, you gotta make a decision and make one fast because I can't keep seeing you hurt like this.

Aniya is never going to admit that she did you wrong."

"But, why mom? Why? I've been there for her since day one, and she shitted on me. She brought me into her home just to break me. To disrespect me and to have her family disrespect me. Mom, she knew I ain't have anything and she still did me dirty. What kind of person does that? I never would have done to her what she did to me."

"I understand baby, but people like that won't have no good coming to them. Believe me, God sees all, and what she did to you will come back on her tenfold. I just need you to forgive her and let go of the hurt and anger so that you can receive your blessings."

My mother was right. As much as I didn't want to admit it at the time, she was right. There had been so many times that I wanted to tag Aniya in a post and put her on blast for being the fake person that I thought she was, but I decided against it. We both had a brand to protect and, nine times out of ten, I would be the only one getting backlash, considering my name was already shit in the industry.

I won't lie and say that me and her never tried to talk about the situation, but it didn't work. I just remember lashing out.

"I was miserable in New York. Every time I looked, yawl were judging me. My clothes weren't good enough. The way I talked wasn't good enough. When I left the house, I was being talked about. Your mother was ignorant to me the entire time I lived there, and I had to deal with that. I didn't say anything because I didn't want to be that disrespectful Annemarie that everyone expected me to be. I wanted to change, and I did change."

"Sis, I'm sorry you had to go through that. I didn't know that they were doing that to you. No one called me about anything. Why didn't you call me and tell me?" she asked.

It was confusing for Aniya to say no one called her and said anything, but then say that every time she looked her family was calling me and complaining about me. It just seemed as though no matter how much we talked, there was never a solution. It was like she was afraid to actually let her guard down and be a good friend.

Nevertheless, I refused to take all the pain, hurt, and anger that I had towards her in the new year. So, I wrote her and let everything out.

Me: I don't wanna take this burden, hate, and hurt into the new year, so I feel like now is the best time to just lay everything out on the table. I know that we talked the last time I came to NY, but I still don't feel like much was accomplished. Maybe it was because I didn't let everything out or say everything I needed to say. Over the years, I was always team Aniya.

Even after the mishap with Spider, I gave you a chance. I supported you %1000 and you always made me feel beneath you. You always made it clear that in your eyes you were better than me. & no, you never said it flat out, but your actions and the way you worded things said it for you. Whenever I tried to be great, you made sure you had to outdo me. You made sure you had to let your accomplishments be known.

The entire Mitch situation, I felt like you were happy the way he disrespected me. He

301

made it known that he believed in you more than me and, in so many words, he said it. When I told you I had another designer that was willing to work with me, you had to let it be known that Mitch was doing your web series for free. When I signed to Mrs. Clark, you signed to Vick, and I felt like it was just to make sure I didn't outdo you.

I never once threw anything in your face to gloat or make you feel like I was better than you. I've learned that if it isn't about Aniya, then it doesn't matter. Another main situation, I came to NY to better myself and left with hate in my heart, something I left Jersey with. The very first time I was homeless, my aunt tortured me. I wasn't allowed to eat, she took my clothes and made me take cold showers whenever I tried to take a nap. I went to school stinking because I had on the same pair of underwear for a week. All because my aunt would steal my clothes.

I was tormented there. Knowing that there were similarities when I moved with your mother made it worse. Not only that, but I've noticed when I lived with you, it was a lot of tension between me and you. I couldn't understand why. I couldn't understand what it was about me that bothered yawl so bad.

Now, here I am having to deal with the fact that I never had the chance to defend myself or speak up for myself. I have to sit back and deal with the things that were said about me because it's your family. Whenever something was done to me, an excuse was made for the person that did it, but if yawl felt like I did something. An excuse couldn't be made for me. It was Reds is selfish, Reds is ungrateful, Reds is bitter, Reds has demons of her own, Reds is this, and Reds is that.

Every time I looked, they were calling you about something or you were popping up in Tims or sneakers. The only people that treated me with respect was James and his nephew Wakeem. I left because I knew that either me and you were going to fight or me and Asia. I could see me disrespecting your mother because I could no longer take the disrespect. So, I left because I wasn't that person anymore.

I wasn't that angry person anymore. I was no longer the person that needed to solve things physically anymore. I never said much before because regardless of how much I say, you don't see what I see. Then, it's like because yawl go to church, everything you do to people it's okay. When I don't answer the phone, it's not to ignore you. it's because I know that I am still growing and learning and, right now, I have a lot of hurt that turned into hate. I don't know what 2018 holds for our friendship.

I really don't know. But I couldn't go into the new year acting like everything was okay. I believe you care about me, Aniya, you just don't know how to show it. I believe you want to have a friendship with me, but you're afraid of something. I know a couple times you said you do love me, but I just couldn't see myself going into the new year *without being upfront. I could have done this over the phone, but you have a tendency of over-talking me. This is not to disrespect you or make you feel like I'm talking down on you. This is simply my feelings.*

I felt such a relief when I sent off that message on Facebook. I had so much bottled up in me over the months that I was only hurting myself and, I knew that sooner or later, I would have to release all that I was feeling, and that's what I did. I needed to let her know what was bothering me and why I backed off the way that I did. For once, I finally realized that I was changing.

Aniya: *Well I for one am glad that you told me what your true feelings were. For one Red, I didn't sign to Vick because u signed to Mrs. Clark. I came to you with that because if u were going back in the game, I wanted to be right there with you but not signing to the same person. You take what I do and see it as competition, but all I was doing is trying to take over the game with you like we did before. Thought we were doing it together.*

I'm not upset about how you feel towards me or my family, and church has nothing to do with that. We ain't perfect and don't try to be. I'm more than 10 years older than you and the way we think are totally different. I promised myself that this new year I was letting go past hurts, bitter ways, raunchy attitudes that I had against people that have hurt me from the past up until my future.

It's toxic to be stressed trying to figure out if someone is mad at you. There is no more that I could say or do to show you that I meant what I said to you and, trust me, I know I have a habit of talking over people. That's one of my big problems, but I'll work on that on my behalf. Now, I know you're still holding ill feelings toward my mother and sister and I see the things you say about them. I bite my tongue because I know they did u wrong from what you told me and you're just speaking your real feelings because it happened to you.

I would be lying if I say that it didn't bother me because at the end of the day, that's still my mother and I ain't got but one. She might be a bitch and a horrible person to someone else but, to me, that's still my mother, my queen. I do respect you for being respectful when u do post about your pain and hurt here, but I won't be in your way for 2018.

I'm always gon love you and I don't use that word lightly but, if you still harboring bad vibes against me, then I'll fall back. I can't keep apologizing and trying to convince you that I truly want you to win. If my family and I have caused u that much pain to a point it still bothers you this much after a lil time, then we need to be out your way.

I pray that you will believe that I was being truthful about loving you and wanting our friendship to work. Happy New Year Reds, and I pray that this new year coming will take you higher than anyone could imagine. I will always be a phone call away. I'm not giving up on us but, right now, you need your space to see what you want to do.

I won't call or text because you make me believe that you think I'm being fake and I'm far from that. My focus point will be on me, my home life, and work. 2018 for me is to let everything go cuz I can't afford to stress over things I have done or that's been done to me because the shit will drive u crazy.

I want you to never change who you are because you are a sweet genuine person. For the last time for 2017, I'm sorry for any wrong that I have done to you and I pray God lifts this burden off your shoulders because you deserve happiness. I'll be right here if you need me.

When I read Aniya's response, it made me angry. I literally had to calm myself down before responding. It never failed; she was always copping a plea, and here I was being honest with her about the way that I was feeling. I didn't expect her to kiss my ass, but I also didn't expect her to try and play victim, as if the things I was saying were false. Yes, she did apologize, but why apologize and then go right back to shooting shots at me on Facebook? Why apologize if you're just going to keep doing me dirty?

I had never posted anything about her mother or sister on Facebook, so why assume that? The only thing I posted about was me having a terrible time in New York. Everything she wrote annoyed me because she made it seem like she had done nothing wrong, and she was only apologizing because I was hurt. That just didn't fly with me, and I couldn't swallow that. I was fucked up over how she did me, and the shit was eating at me every damn day. Then to have people looking at me sideways because I fell back from her was wrong on so many levels. Instead of being truthful about how she did me she played the victim and I couldn't let that slide.

Me: *Well, I appreciate what you said. But what I won't take is you saying that after a little time, I'm still bothered, as if I should be over it because it's not that big of a deal in your eyes. As far as you saying it bothers you when I post about them, that's your problem and the guilt of you knowing they did me wrong because not once have I bluntly put out there anything about them.*

I won't sugarcoat anything because not once I have disrespected them when I made my posts or when I vented. You keep saying your family isn't perfect and y'all don't try to be, but that's a lie. Maybe you're not use to someone actually speaking up about the wrongdoing. Moving on, you're making it seem as though I'm in competition with you when, in all reality, we both know that's not the truth.

I'm not the only one who sees it, but I won't even involve other people because this is between me and you. This is where we agree to disagree, and I'll take it just as that. Maybe I should have said call me once you read the message and actually thought about it before responding because the way you worded things were a little off. But either way, I won't be in your way for 2018 either and I wish you much success, happiness, and good health.

The conversation didn't go how I expected it to. I didn't expect it to be all peaches and cream, but I was seriously trying to make a breakthrough to Aniya. Like, you hurt me. Why would you hurt me the way that you did when I was riding with you? I was ten toes down for you. I was willing to beat any bitch or nigga ass when it came to Aniya, and I didn't receive any of it back in return. The only thing I got was her doing me dirty and, because she allowed me to stay with her, everything she did to me was supposed to be pushed to the side?

Aniya: *Yea they could've been a lil off cuz I was just waking up when I saw it and was typing with the phone and I see mad typos. Trying to respond to everything you said I got side track but, as you saw, I said thanks for being respectful about it. Of course, I'm gon feel some kind of way because it's still my family, just as well you would feel the same way about yours. They were wrong and I know that and I never said different. I would've rather talked to you over the phone about it, so I could be clear on a few things and I never said you were in competition with me. I said I didn't want you to look at it as if I was in competition because I signed to Vick.*

I went to you and asked you was it a good idea, and I kept saying I was scared to sign again and you encouraged me. While I'm looking to you for comfort in some of the decisions I make, it came off as if I was trying to outshine you. That's crazy if that's what anyone thinks. I promise I'm not mad about it cuz I know I have a lot to work on with me. This is why I fear opening up to someone because when I do, it don't look like the relationship would last.

I have a lot of personal issues that I'm scared to relive because of how painful it was. and that was an error when I said lil time, I meant all this time when I mentioned that line as well. Yea, I'm probably all over the place again but trying to speak on everything you posted in here. I'm only falling back because I want to give you time to heal. You can take as much time as you need. I wasn't rushing it like as if you needed to get over things right away. No, that's not what I mean.

Wat I said is I don't want to keep trying and you still holding on to your hurt because damage was done, so I have to give you that *space for you to heal and not confuse things. I'm hoping 2018 we will have enough space and come together and be stronger and better friends. I'm learning what it takes to be a friend and I will be doing that, so I won't ruin anymore relationships. With all my past hurts, it's hard for me to open up and that's unfair to people that I let in my life because yawl are only seeing the tough side that I keep to hide the hurt and pain that I really have deep inside of me. One of these days, I will sit down and tell you everything, even shit my family don't know when we get in a better place. I'm still going to support you. This is not to end what we have, it's just to give each other the space so we can heal. you from being hurt by a friend, and me healing from causing the hurt and trying to become better. I'm not going anywhere and, even if its two years from now, I'll still be here.*

I didn't care about her last response because she turned it into a situation about her. It wasn't that I was being selfish. It was just that I was tired of taking her bullshit. I was tired of having to accept the fact that she did me wrong because that's basically what she was saying. No one gave me any passes. No matter what it was that I'd done or that somebody thought I did, I had somebody's foot in my neck. I was becoming a different person, and I refused for anyone to downplay me or make me feel like I was the problem or that I was taking a situation overboard.

Aniya had proved to me long ago that she wasn't for me, but I kept fighting for our friendship. I kept fighting for her sistership. I kept fighting for her to give me the same loyalty and love that I showed her as a friend and as a sister. I understood that she was hurt. I understood that she may have been through some fucked up shit, but taking out on me what she wished she should've done to others was wrong. I was her shadow. I was her ace boon coon, and I wished anybody would come for her while I was around, or it was going to be problems. It was true; she didn't know how to be a friend, nor did she know how to be a sister and, even with me knowing this, I continued to fight for our friendship.

I wanted her to see that I was rocking it out with her. I wanted her to see that it was okay for her to open up to me. I wanted her to see that it was okay for her to show me that soft side. I wanted her to see that it was okay to let her guard down. I wanted her to see that it was okay to be herself with me. I know this shit sounds gay as hell, but I really wanted her to see that I was true to her. I had never told her business and, as bad as I had every right to, I didn't.

I never downplayed her. I never called her stupid. I never made her feel like a decision she was making or going to make was bad. I supported her in everything she did and wanted to do. All I asked for was the same in return but, no matter how much I fought, the truth was there, and it wasn't good.

We ended up talking on the phone after exchanging Facebook messages and I still felt bitter after we hung up. She did admit to how she was jealous of me and Asia's relationship, but that was the only thing I truly believed out of all the things that she had said. It was still the same outcome. Me sharing my truth and her giving me excuses in return. My life wasn't a lie. I wasn't here to please people. My truth was my truth, and I felt like she played on that to have more in common with me.

For years, she told me how she didn't know how it felt to be homeless or to be without. She would tell me how she didn't know what it was like to have a bill cut off or what it was like to not have money. Now, all of a sudden, she comes to me saying she was homeless before and she was raped? That was just a pill I couldn't swallow. I couldn't rock with someone who pretended to go through what I went through. That shit broke me. It took me several years to be able to sleep at night. It took me several years to actually be stable and I'm still not.

It took me several years to be able to finally push the pain I'd endured to the side and just live life. But, that was the difference between me and Aniya. She was a storyteller, and I told my story.

64

Friend or Foe: The Beginning of the End of Toxic Friendships

WHEN I LET OUT HOW I TRULY FELT TO ANIYA, I ALSO let out how I truly felt to Porsha. I hated that we ended, but how much more could I take? Every time we went out, I was the odd ball out of the bunch because I was a big girl and my skin was dark. One of her homegirls even told me that I was clashing them.

"Damn, girl you the only dark skinned one out of the bunch, and the biggest one. You fucking up the squad goals."

That shit hurt my soul and, no, I didn't say anything because my loyalty was so deep for Porsha that I just didn't want to mess anything up because she was my only real friend. It was because of her that I was getting out, actually having a life. I just didn't want to mess that up. We had some bomb ass memories and I wanted to have more, but my heart and mind wouldn't allow me to go on any further.

Reds: *I didn't care to before, but the new year is rolling in and I don't want any burden, pain, or hurt on me if I can stop it. The last time I stopped talking to you, mommie told me you reached out to her. I didn't care because I knew you knew why I stopped talking to you. Porsche, when you and my brother broke up, he wanted me to stop being friends with you. I told him no, I wasn't going to do that. You know how I felt about my brother. I was team jay all the way. I was always ready to knock someone's head off for him, but I told him no because you were the only girlfriend he had that decided to figure out why I always stayed in the room. You didn't judge me, but you helped me. You took me to my first bar, my first college party, my first club, I had my first drink with you, I smoked weed for the first time with you, I attended my very first house party with you. I felt alive. I was living my teenage life at the age of 22/23.*

What hurt the most is the things that were said about me. Alyssa made it clear that I was clashing yawl style because I wasn't natural. She made a dark-skinned comment and a fat joke comment when we went out to our last college party. I never once heard you defend me. When I called you my sister. I meant it, regardless if we shared the same blood or not. I didn't have my own sisters and you were that big sister figure to me. But it was like it was an insult to you for you to say it back. No matter what it was that you needed, I was there. I let you borrow money before and not once have I ever asked for it back. Your bday party that you had at Alyssa house, me and Zy were the only girls who didn't get any play because we were big. I knew that truth, but I continued to have a good time because it was your day. The same with your hotel party. Everyone had a dude but me. Which was fine because I wanted you to have a good time. When your cousin was all over ya dude after you had passed out. I let it be known the shit was *fucked up. And I told you the next day. On my celebration day, I bought you an early bday cake because I knew I wasn't going to have the money later. When we went to the spot, I only had $26 to my name but, when you wanted a drink and something to eat, I told you to get whatever and spent my last on you with no problem. It bothered me when you wasted the drink and let Chris and his friends eat your food. But, I didn't say anything because it was your day. When you got a boyfriend, I supported you. Because I knew your pain and hurt. We had so much in common and I wanted you to be happy so bad because you deserved it. When you got with him, you changed. What bothered me was when you always would say you didn't come to Bridgeton but, when you got with him, you had no issue with coming to Bridgeton. I never once said anything when my mother told me she saw him with another female. I knew I was your friend and I should've been honest, but I had never seen you so happy before so I kept my* *mouth shut. When I would look at your snap and see you having house gatherings, going out to bars and so on, all you had to do was ask did I want to go. I may have declined but it was about the thought. That's all I wanted was for you to care about me as much as I cared about you. Even after we stopped being cool, I see how you went to Philly even after the many times I said we should go and you like, nah, I don't do that anymore. I can see the fakeness with the people you hang out with. Family or not, I see it because I live it and it bothered me so much because I thought you would realize the genuine person I was and treat me as one of your sisters. I'm not writing this, so we can be friends again. I'm just writing this to let you know how and why I felt the way I did. I still love you like a sister because you helped me experience things I would have never experienced if you wouldn't have gotten me out of my room. I can never forget that.*

Porsha: *Some of this isn't facts but I'ma let you have it because I been stopped caring. For multiple reasons. But, let me clarify something, I'm the realest person a lot of mfs will ever meet. I bend over backwards for people and never ask for anything back. You know the things I've done for you but, of course, it's forgotten because you've done some things for me. But that's neither here nor there. I reached out to your mom this time when you stopped speaking to me too, and she basically put the blame all on me so I went on about my business. To know you were supposed to be my friend, sister, or whatever and you didn't speak up when she said she seen MY BOYFRIEND with another female shows your loyalty. Whether or not you've heard it or not, I've taken up for you more times than none and that's real. I don't have to speak about what I've done or who I've done it for because I don't owe anyone an explanation. I stopped calling you sister the first time I heard you tell your friend in New York I was your friend. But, that title shit don't mean anything because the bond was there. Or so*

I thought it was. I'm not even with Chris anymore but you have to respect people's relationships, you have to understand when someone is tied down, there's things they can and cannot do anymore. Period. And since we are being perfectly honest, I've always hated how your family treats you, that's why I didn't like coming over there. Because I can't be fake. And also, as I've explained before, I don't drive to a lot of places I go to, nor am I the one making the plans so I can't always include you. I have a lot of friends and you knew that. And we all know a lot of people. I can't help that. I didn't ever not invite you because I just didn't want you to come and, if that was the case, I would've said so. Just like yourself, I never been the one to bite my tongue and you know that as well. With all of that being said, I hope 2018 and every other year after that is a good year for you. I'm still proud of everything you have accomplished and everything you will accomplish. I still tell people my friend is an author. And I'll never throw dirt on your name like you've done mine. I'll never throw shade at you on these social sites like you've done to me. And I'll never forget our memories. Goodbye.

Reds: *The goodbye wasn't needed because I said my intentions aren't to be friends with you anymore. Everything I said was true but, of course, because you don't agree with it, it's not facts. I'm not here to go back and forth. I said what I said and meant it. I wasn't about to tell you anything about YOUR BOYFRIEND because you were head over hills for him. What I said wouldn't have mattered. & loyalty? I would rather you not speak upon my loyalty. Because you still hang out with the very cousin that had your male friend grab her bare ass and was hugged up with each other at your hotel party. I said one thing about you on snap, and I couldn't care less if you felt like anything else was about you. You act too perfect as if you never shitted on me, but that's okayy. There ain't no need to respond because you don't agree with what I said,* *and I don't agree what you're saying. You can delete and block me, honestly. Be blessed*

The way shit ended was fucked up, but it was needed. Whenever I wanted to move on with my life, I was the one in the wrong for wanting to do so. I was called fake or disloyal, but it was all good when I was dealing with the way they were treating me. I won't front and act like I didn't cry because I did. It hurt to lose somebody that I truly cared for. But, I couldn't constantly take being talked down to because I was fat or because my skin was darker than everyone she hung out with. Porsha had a way of making someone feel like they were the suspect and she was the victim. I had witnessed it one too many times when she and her other friends fell out. I would see exactly the way things went down and she would swear she never did anything, but I called her out on it. I was her friend and I was riding with her until the end, rather she was right or wrong.

65

Speaking My Truth: Connecting More With The Woman Who Birthed Me

I DIDN'T REVEAL THE TRUE STORY BEHIND MY molestation until I was twenty-four. I remember I was sitting on my sister's bed and my mother was sitting on the couch. I told her how my brother and sister touched me, and she looked at me like I was crazy. She couldn't believe what I was saying and she broke down crying.

"That's why you so fucked up now because they just used and abused you," my mother broke down crying.

My mother had been through a lot. On top of dealing with the bullshit I took her through with these no-good ass niggas, she was also dealing with shit from my oldest sister Dani. Dani had been fucking since she was eleven years old and, by the time she was fourteen, she had slept with over twenty-five men. Not only that but, in her adult years, she started snorting coke, popping pills, and drinking something serious.

Linette was also a problem. My mother had custody of all three of Linette's kids, whom were all by her cousins. It was stressful for my mother to not have a life but cater to children who weren't hers. My mother had given up her entire life to cater to us. Back then, my mother was getting raped by my father's father, beat by her mother, and raped by the men that her mother brought around, and beat on by my father. Her mother was an alcoholic, and my father was a coke head and I didn't know that until I was twenty-one years old. I knew that my father was an alcoholic back then, but being on coke? I had no idea.

I was the first person that my mother told about the abuse she endured. She told me about how when she didn't give sex to my father, he would just take it. He would beat on her until she was a bloody pulp, and he had cheated on her with over seventy women. She told me how she had no one to turn to because everyone thought she was lying. Her family and his family hated her because she was light skinned. I was broken for her. I wanted to kill everyone that had harmed her. I wanted to torture them the way they tortured her. When my father's father died, I was glad that he was dead. When my mother's mother died, I was glad she was dead.

They messed my mother up mentally. To this day, she can't sleep at night. To this day, she has panic attacks. To this day, she's afraid of the dark. To this day, she hates loud noises. To this day, she gets so scared at any sort of violence. To this day, she is depressed at times because what they did to her took over her life. So, when I told my mother that I was molested, it brought back bad memories for her.

"I knew that you had been through something, but I wanted you to be ready to tell me," she said.

This may seem unreal to a lot, but my mother has a third eye. She has visions of what is going to happen before they already happen. That's why she didn't want me to go out that night I got raped. I didn't listen to her when I should have, but I can't change the past. Everyone always asks why me and my mother is so close the way we are. I tell them because she's my best friend. I can tell her anything and not be judged. Regardless, of what happened in the past when I felt like she didn't protect me when my father disrespected me, I understand why she didn't.

She was afraid, and I couldn't blame her. I love my mother to pieces. Through the ups and downs. Through thick and thin. She's my strength, and I'm hers. She's my backbone, and I'm hers. She's my rock, and I'm hers.

66

Feeling Unappreciated

I THOUGHT THINGS WOULD HAVE GOTTEN BETTER, BUT they didn't. I was extremely stressed out. I was back gaining weight, and everything about life, well, my life, was just fucked up. I couldn't stand my sister, and I couldn't stand living there. Although I was signed to Mrs. Clark, I still wasn't happy. I was watching my mother stress but, most of the times, she caused it on herself because she just wouldn't let go of the things she needed to let go.

My sister was constantly getting paid every week and giving her paycheck up to a nigga that didn't give a fuck about her, but he knew that if he gave her a little dick, then that would result into him getting her money. The house was always without food, the bills were back, and I was sleeping on a roach infested couch. But, no one cared. Everyone walked around like the way we were living wasn't a problem.

I was tired of living in the ghetto. I was tired of having to struggle. It seemed like everyone was okay with where they were, and I was tired of that. I would literally wake up because roaches were crawling on me. I couldn't sit a plate of food or a cup of juice down without seeing a roach in it. I was sleeping in the living room and my dresser was a damn bookstand. The bathroom was in the living room and, whenever somebody took a shit or if they were just a stank individual in general, I was the one smelling it first.

I was tired. Sick and tired of being sick and tired. I wished that I had done right by the money I was making back then because then maybe, just maybe, I would have been in a better predicament. I tried talking to my mother, but she always felt like I was belittling them or talking down to them.

What was wrong with wanting better? I realized that my mother was afraid of me being on my own because she didn't want me to leave her but, regardless if I was on my own or not, that was never going to happen. I was just tired of being thrown out of apartments and houses. Tired of wondering when my next meal was going to come. But, no matter how tired I was, things just never got better because there was an eviction noticed slapped right on Linette's door and, once again, we had to find another place to stay.

So, who went apartment hunting? My mother. Like always, she was the one handling all the business while other people sat on their ass. I didn't even know she had found a place until Linette said something about it.

"Mom, did you tell her?" she asked.

"No," she responded.

"Tell me what?" I was already aggravated.

"We found a place," Linette revealed.

"Oh, that's nice. Do I get a room?" I asked.

Both Linette and my mom were looking like a deer in headlights. They hadn't even considered giving me a room and that shit broke me. I was the one giving up my money to help out and I couldn't even get a room?

"Mommy want you to be comfortable, so I'm going to get you a pull-out couch."

All I could do was walk away after she said that. A pull-out couch? I wasn't good enough for a room, but I was good enough for a pull-out couch? That shit hurt, and that was something I never forgave either one of them for so, when the day came for them to move, I didn't help with shit. I sat my fat ass on that same roach infested couch and played the game the entire time.

Shanda helped them move and, that night, she came to me and asked me did I want to come stay the night at her house. I had already assumed that my mom had talked to her, but Shanda said she didn't. She said she knew that I was uncomfortable, and she wanted me to be comfortable. I was still angry and hurt, but I did finally get up and pack my bags. So, up until this point, I was still living with my nephew's mother.

67

Friend or Foe: The Beginning of The End of A Toxic Friendship

I HAD FINALLY REVEALED THAT I WAS GOING TO BE releasing my memoir, and I had gotten so much positive support and feedback. But, low and behold, there was hell of shade thrown at me from a lot of people, including Aniya, and I had only known that due to a mutual friend telling me that her statuses were about me. I didn't trip because she wasn't the only one throwing shade, and I still didn't follow Aniya and I didn't bother to look at her page but, me knowing how jealous she got whenever I got a little shine, I could just imagine what was on her page, so I took it upon myself to update a general status knowing that it would hurt a guilty soul.

Aniya: *So, I just so happen to come across your post and I'm saying dang, I haven't* *spoken to her in a min so who she talking bout but, when I look at my post that I shared from my uncle speaking this morning, I'm like I know she's not thinking that was about her. Listen, I see wat it is. You don't mess with me, cool. We can dead whatever it is we had, no love lost.*

You still got stuff at my crib. I can never hate on u because I want u to do good but if that's what you believe, then we need to not be friends cuz this is enough and I don't play the fb games. I always come to u if I feel something. Fb can't help me. Last, u said u would hit me up but come on, some of what u posted today really look like u coming at me and why? when u got my number and address to step to me personally or call me. I call your mom to check on u and all, so it's not me. When you're here, your good but, when you leave, it's another problem that idk bout. Bipolar kind of stuff.

When I read the message, I had to pray before I responded. I had to pray because Aniya just swore she was so hard. She swore that I was scared of her.

It was like she wanted me to be scared of her. She wanted me to be that same Reds that wouldn't say shit and would just allow people to talk. Every time I looked, she was throwing her weight around. It became annoying, and I sure as hell wasn't the one for it. There had been plenty of times that she quote on quote had a problem with me and would never say anything to me, so for her to say that she always came to me whenever she felt someway was untrue.

I also didn't like how she mentioned you still got stuff at my crib. Like, what exactly did that mean? That was one of the main reasons why I didn't play anyone, especially females, too close because what point was she trying to prove? The only thing that I had left at her house was a pair of sneakers, a pair of baby doll shoes, and some bedroom slippers, along with some paperwork. She was making it seem as though I had a whole damn storage at her house.

I had given Aniya multiple chances to buck, and the way she had it out was that I was this punk ass bitch. She was the first one to say she didn't do the Facebook games, but the main one updating indirect statuses whenever she felt a way. When I was in New York for the last time, I came in sneakers since everyone had a problem with Reds. I came alone, and I was ready for anything. Rather I got my ass beat or rather I beat ass, I was there by myself ready for whatever. So, for her to say I had her address as if I was scared was just beyond me. I didn't need to throw my weight around, nor did I need to make it known that I was about that life time and time again to prove anything. It was annoying for her to think or make every situation about her as if she was just that important, and I just had to let it be known that she wasn't.

Me: *First off, I don't even follow you on Facebook. I don't see what you post unless I go directly to your page. So, because I mention the literary industry you automatically think it's about you? Whenever I make a post, you feel like it's about you, and that's not my problem. You can see whatever you want. Again, that's not my problem.*

I know I still got stuff at your house. What's your point? Like, don't ever make it seem like I'm scared to come to you if I have an issue. I said what I said to you plenty of times. I'm not about to mess up my brand to come at you on FB. So, this entire message you wrote me wasn't needed because if you ain't the one throwing shots at me, then don't feel no way. I said I would reach out. I got several books I'm writing, I'm in three different contracts that I need to fulfill, and I'm in the process of moving in my house. I haven't been talking to no one. So, whatever you feel is on you.

The moment I checked her, her entire attitude changed. She directed the conversation on her, which was what she wanted in the first place. It was like she needed to get my attention by any means, and all she had to do was say she wanted my attention. If I wasn't entertaining Aniya, then she was going to do any and everything in her power for me to entertain her. I realized long ago that something was truly wrong with Aniya, Hell, something was truly wrong with me, but there was a different type of something wrong with her. She did any and everything for attention, and that was just someone I could no longer associate myself with. I was trying my hardest to remain focus and positive, and being friends with her was stressing me out more than it was helping me.

I shared the messages with my friend Nicki and all she could do was shake her head, but her advice to me was on point.

"Sis, she did whatever she could to get you to talk to her. I read your status and nothing was directed towards her; she just wanted a reason to hop in your inbox because you wasn't talking to her. I just wish she leave you alone and let you be great."

Nicki was right. I wasn't speaking to Aniya because I was focused on my own thing and, whenever me and her spoke, it knocked me off my focus because she was so negative. I wasn't sure if it was intentional, but everything seemed so cold and negative whenever we talked, and I couldn't deal with that. Then, I noticed that she didn't reach out because I was her *lil sis* or that she wanted to see how I was doing. She only reached out to know the moves I was making and to let me know the moves she was making and, when she couldn't get to me, she would reach out to my mother and I knew that was only to see how our attitudes towards her would be.

I realized just how envious Aniya was not after I got signed to Mrs. Clark, but when Shyanna got a reality show TV deal. She called me and she was pissed the fuck off, and I honestly couldn't believe how she could be so angry because someone else was making it.

"How the fuck did she get a deal? That bitch is a nobody. I got more drama than her shit, they need to put me up there."

"A lot of doors open when you're signed to certain people. You can't knock her hustle. Me, personally, I couldn't do it because I'll be beating bitches' asses every episode."

"I just don't get it. I got more books out than her, and I got more shit under my belt. I got drama if they want drama! Hell, even you got more books out than her. They should've picked us to be on TV. Like damn, when we gon' get our break?"

It was nothing but venom spewing off Aniya's tongue, and I couldn't understand because it was enough out here for all of us to eat. We were all connected to some major people, so why be mad at the next one for making moves? We all were gifted and talented, so why be so angry at Shyanna for getting the deal of a lifetime? Granted, we both had our thoughts about Shyanna at times, but I knew what it was like to struggle and fall in the industry. I was glad that Shyanna was making it, even if I felt like she needed to be humble at times. But, despite that, I wanted someone to finally speak up about how shady the industry was, and she was the one that was able to do so and have it be on national television. There was no way I was going to knock her for being successful. She deserved every bit of shine that she was getting, and even when myself, Aniya, and Shyanna had a three-way call I made sure to encourage Shyanna to do the reality show even after she had made the decision not to.

Aniya, on the other hand, just wasn't feeling Shyanna's success. Which was why she started doing live shows every Friday, to show people she brought the drama. It was sad, but what could I say? Shyanna adored Aniya and she praised her every chance she got. The feelings just weren't mutual on Aniya's end. She talked about Shyanna like a dog, and I won't front; I made my comments too, but I stopped once I realized just how good of a person Shyanna really was; she was just misunderstood, just like I was. I had only talked to Shyanna on the phone a couple of times, but I knew that she wasn't the person I thought she was. I learned that she really was a good person that had just been fucked over one too many times, and she just wasn't beat for any bullshit.

Aniya even went as far as to telling me that Shyanna didn't write her own books, which was why they got out so fast. I was shocked, but that's what happen when someone put their trust in the wrong person. She sent me a screenshot that had a small conversation between them.

Shyanna: *You want me to find another author?*

Aniya: *Nah, let me see what's going on with my computer first.*

Shyanna: *Okay.*

Shyanna: *Hey sis. I got my assistant taking care of everything. Thank you so much, and I will call you soon.*

Aniya: *Okay honey.*

Apparently, Shyanna had a release coming out which wasn't finished yet and she needed Aniya to write the book for her, considering she types fast and the book was supposed to be between forty to forty-five thousand words. Now, right after they messaged each other on Facebook, Aniya called me, and we had an entire conversation about it. She told me she knew that something was up because Shyanna wrote her books too fast. I made sure not to speak on it too much because I didn't want to be a part of any of the Facebook drama if Shyanna found out that she told me about her not writing her own books.

Not only did I know that, but I also knew how Shyanna would call Aniya, asking her for money. Well, in Aniya's words, she was begging but, from what I knew about Shyanna, she wasn't begging for anything. I was also sent Shyanna's porn video by Aniya, when I didn't even know she had a porn video out. I also didn't know that Shyanna's boyfriend had a baby mom that was giving her problems. Shyanna wanted Aniya to report the girl's Facebook page until it was shut down because the girl and her friends put out a porn video of him jerking off and having his fingers places they shouldn't be.

So, to find out that Shyanna was making statuses about me because she thought I was fake by the way Aniya portrayed me to be was baffling. I may be a lot of things, but fake isn't one of them. I was fucked over, so I shut down instead of lashing out how everyone expected me to. I know people are like, so you're telling stuff she told you to prove a point? Nah, I'm speaking on certain things to let people know that everything that glitters isn't gold and to not believe all the hype because even salt looks like sugar. I know people are like, well, she told you that stuff because yawl were best friends. If that was the case, why tell people anything I so called said about them, IF we were *best friends*? Why have people inboxing me saying what they heard I said about them? When SHE was the only one who knew such things about similar situations?

So, if I'm such a fake ass bitch that talks about everyone, then how do I know certain stuff? Because Shyanna never talked to me on a personal level. She barely liked me so, telling me her business wasn't an option and the stuff she'd put on Facebook was not the stuff that I was told. Have I ever talked about anyone? Hell yea. Both me and Aniya spoke on a lot. But, to put me out as if I said all this negative stuff about everyone just to save face is sad.

However, I couldn't get mad at Shyanna for admiring and looking up to Aniya because that was me at one point. I couldn't get mad at Shyanna for her feeling the way she did about me because she was riding with her friend. I couldn't get mad at Shyanna for sharing such secrets with Aniya because she had a lot of dirt on me too, but the difference was I didn't give the slightest fuck about her airing my dirty laundry. I was a loyal friend but, the moment you try to hurt me, I was coming from your jugular. Never drive a loyal person to the point where they no longer cared. I knew just as much about her as she knew about me, if not more and, after all she had taken me through and done to me, if she ever wanted to go there, I would go right there with her if she pushed me to that limit.

Terry even said her few choice words about me and, again, I couldn't be mad because I was portrayed a certain way. She came to me so called confronting me about what she heard, and I knew that Aniya had told her something because Aniya was the only person that knew that I felt like Terry was controlling but, then again, she still had to make me look bad. Telling everything I so called said but not one peep about anything she said.

I was aware of Terry not liking me and that's okay. I didn't have anything bad to say about her because she helped me at my lowest. Yea, she comes off as it's either her way or the highway and that's not how I get down because I have one mother and her name is Maria. I felt like that was the only reason we actually clashed because I didn't do as she said, which came off as controlling. But, it was because of her that I was able to get a few more covers done at the time I needed them. Still to this day, I owe her sixty dollars and, regardless if we're cool or not, she's going to get that sixty dollars back because she didn't have to take money out of her home to help me.

It wasn't her obligation to help me through my struggle, but she did. Even though she bad mouthed me on Facebook, I'm never going to forget the words she spoke to me.

I'm good. I want you to be good. That's how you pay me back.

The realest shit that ever came from somebody who disliked me. Regardless of how much we clashed or how much was said, she wanted me to be good. That was her main focus: 'Reds, I want you to be good', and that's something I'm never going to forget.

So, for all that are reading my memoir and wondering are me and Aniya still friends? No, we're not, but I was cordial with her to an extent before things ended completely. I will never mess up my brand to come at her or any other author because I worked too hard to get to where I am today. I know people are probably reading this like bitch, you don't have a brand. Well, believe it or not, I do, and I refuse to jeopardize it just to Facebook thug.

I also know that people expect me to be full of drama due to the dirt that has already been thrown on my name, and I refuse to give anyone the satisfaction of seeing me come out of character again. No, I didn't delete her and, no, we never fought, although I know deep down she wanted to.

I wish her all the best in the world, in her career, and with her family. I hope God blesses her abundantly. I hope that each and every one of her books hit the best sellers. I hope that everything she wants in life at this point comes true. No matter how much wrong she has done to me, I will never wish her harm or not wish her success. It's way too many black women downing one another as it is, and I just won't be one of them.

Some people may read this and think I'm fake and disloyal because how can I stop being cool with someone who *took me in*? Or how can I stop being cool with someone who brought me around their *family*? However, I honestly don't care how anyone feels about me protecting my peace. No one was there to experience what I did, so all people are going by is her side of the story. There's a difference between genuinely helping someone, helping someone because you pity them, and helping someone so you can throw it in their face later.

A real friend wouldn't kick their friend when they're down. When my books weren't hitting the bestseller's list, Aniya made it her business to send me a screenshot of her book on the bestseller's list when we were in the middle of having a heart to heart. When my books weren't selling and I was struggling to make ends meet, Aniya didn't hesitate to send me screenshots of the thousands of dollars she was making from her books. When I was depressed and on the verge of suicide, Aniya didn't hesitate to make the conversation about her. When I was getting dragged through the industry, not once did Aniya defend me, but she didn't hesitate to send me a screenshot and let me know that I was being talked about. When I fell flat on my face in the industry and I kept trying to bounce back, I got no support from Aniya. The only thing I received was her talking down on me.

I don't care how much one praise the Lord every Sunday. None of that will cover up the type of person someone truly is. I will never forget the disrespectful and hurtful things that were said to me by her and some of her family. I allowed it to eat me up for a long time before I realized the best thing to do was to let go because I was becoming bitter and angry.

So, that's what I did. I silently let our friendship go, and I don't have one ounce of regret. I had a completely different ending to this book, but Aniya couldn't handle that I was no longer speaking to her, and she needed to do something to make herself look like the victim, so she made a live on Facebook and spoke her piece. I never watched the live, but I did receive screenshots from readers and people who knew that I lived in New York with her.

I went to the live because Shyanna shared it. I assumed it was because she wanted me to see it. So, instead of watching it I took it upon myself to read the comments, and I can't even front; it had my blood boiling. It wasn't the live that had me upset because I didn't watch it, it was the comments that were made because everything was one sided. Females that she had talked about was commenting calling me fake, and I laughed because the same way she was talking about me, she had talked about them. It was like the same females we talked about they became cool once me and her stopped being cool. Shyanna made her comments and even went as far as to updating indirect statuses about me, and Aniya commented on them. I guess it was to have me comment and argue, but I didn't even give them my energy.

I didn't trip because Shyanna was only being a loyal friend, and she only had gotten one side of the story. She may read this book and still not believe a damn thing I'm saying, but I don't care. She may read this and call Aniya and be like look at this fake ass bitch talking this bullshit, but I don't care. She may even update a status on Facebook calling me all types of names, but I don't care. This book is not to stop her and Aniya from being friends. That's not my goal nor is that what I want. I'm just simply speaking my truth. People are entitled to believe what they choose to believe. People are entitled to feel the way they want to feel. I just hope she be careful and realize that if Aniya could do what she did to me, just imagine what she could do to her.

I saw people telling her to throw away the things I had left at her house, and I laughed at that too. Because I had lost everything when I was homeless the first time, so losing some bedroom slippers and some paperwork didn't mean a damn thing to me because it could be replaced. People were calling me fat bitches, and I laughed at that too. Because I know I'm fat, that's nothing new. That's everyone's go to when they no longer like me. People were calling me fake, and I laughed at that too. Because everyone that came into my life whether it was male or female I was ten toes down for them, but people get upset when you start to treat them how they treated you.

My friend watched her entire live and called me running everything down to me on what was said. She made it clear that she was glad that I didn't watch it because it was nothing but hate. Aniya spoke on how I called her mother ignorant, which was true, but I said that to Aniya, not Sonya, and it was in a phone conversation when we were discussing what actually went down when I lived with her mother. She said how I didn't respect my mother, but since when? My mother is my best friend, my mother knows everything about me, unlike her mother, my mother doesn't use me for money, my mother doesn't kick me when I'm down so, since when don't I respect my mother?

I assumed she was referring to the argument me and my mother got into while we were on three-way with her, but I had to let them know that none of them was there when I was being dragged on Facebook and that was true.

She spoke on how I walked around her house around her husband in skimpy clothes and, if that was the case, why have me around? She spoke on how I was taking up a whole room with my belongings, which was untrue because like I said, all I had was some bedroom slippers and a pair of sneakers left there. Oh, I also had a synthetic lace front wig, some hair glue, a fitted hat, and some paperwork left there my mistake.

She spoke on how if her family bullied me so much, why did I come back to New York for my birthday. To make that clear, I came back because she was begging to spend my birthday with me. Her daughter even hit me up on Snapchat asking me when I was coming back, and I said I didn't know because it was so much drama. Her exact words were, "You need to just come back because nobody's worried about you."

"Clearly, they are worried, considering my name is in their mouths," I responded.

I immediately called Aniya to let her know what was said before my words got switched up. I ended up going to New York anyway, and I made sure to let Aniya know that I was coming in sneakers, since everyone had a problem with me.

"Reds, I'm not gon' let anything happen to you, but do as you please," she said.

I didn't care what she'd said because no matter how much she called me her little sis, that was still her blood family that had an issue with me from what she told me. So, I went to New York with sneakers and jeans on. I was by myself and ready for whatever. When I got there, Aniya and her husband were standing outside, which was weird.

"Yo, Asia just left. I had to tell my husband that we had to get her out of here because you were on ya way. He came out here, so you would know that wasn't no funny shit going on," she said to me.

I didn't believe her until her husband clarified that Asia did pop up unexpectedly and that Aniya was trying to get her out of there. That same night, we ended up going to Dallas BBQ's, a place that I always wanted to go. I ended up getting drunk, but not as drunk as Aniya thought I was. I remembered everything from that night. I had hella fun, the food was great, and the drinks were great, and I'm not even a drinker. The bill came to $108.94, and we both paid for our own meals. My total was $54.47, and I clarify this because in the live, she explained how she paid for everything. The only thing she paid for was the cab on the way home because she thought I was drunk. I still got the receipt and bank statement to this day.

Moving on, when I got back to Jersey, everything was good, but then I started seeing the indirect statuses, and I'm like damn, I just left so what now? I was tired of the long talks when she was just going to do what she wanted regardless. So, I fell back because it was just tiring. She had hurt me and acted as if she didn't do anything wrong, so I got tired of giving oxygen to a dead situation.

I was also told how she said I tried to split her kids up because of how close I was to her oldest daughter. Like, really? If that was the case, wouldn't she have beat my ass because I was coming between her children? She's a mama bear, so she would have protected her cubs. I was close to her oldest because I knew what it was like to not have anyone to talk to, big sister wise. Her daughter was unhappy and thinking suicide so, before that happened, I was going to do my damn best to get her through whatever it was that she was going through. I refused to see her give up when she had so much potential and so much going for herself. Why on earth would I try to break up a sibling bond and, again, if that was the case, wouldn't she have beat my ass?

I was told how she kept saying that I needed to come get my stuff and how she's not mailing shit, and how she wasn't going to touch me if and when I did come. I was glad she thought I feared her in any way, shape, form, or fashion.

Like, she really had it out there like I was fearful to come back, which was false. She had ample chances to knock my head off and she didn't but, again, she had to put on a show.

I was also told how she said that she was in my city and I didn't do anything, which was completely funny to me because Aniya knew that I had unfollowed her off Facebook, so I couldn't see anything she posted, and I didn't know she was in Atlantic City until my mother told me after their phone conversation.

She tried to make me out to be this punk. Yea, she was in New Jersey, but she wasn't in my city. I live in Bridgeton, New Jersey, which was two hours away from Atlantic City. Anybody who really felt some sort of way would have called me, right? Or at least text, inboxed, or even tagged me on Facebook, right?

Everything she said was to make me look bad and, in the midst of it all, she kept saying how I'm still her little sis, and how she still loves me and never wanted to do what she did. She said how she never wanted to put me on blast, but she ain't put me on blast because not once was I tagged or mentioned in the comments. She always claimed how she didn't do Facebook games, but what did she prove? That she was about Facebook games. She tried her hardest to make me look bad, and it almost worked because people believed her, but all she did was she showed her true colors, not mines. She kept saying how she wanted me to win. How do you want someone to win when every time that person makes a move, you tell them how they shouldn't have done that? How it's going to backfire on them? They ruined their career? You can't take them with you because the people you're associated with can't associate their self with the type of books I write? Stop trying to collaborate with people? Stop signing to people? That's not wanting to see someone win, point blank period.

Now, if I was such a grimy person and I did all this in New York, why on earth didn't no one beat my ass? Why on earth didn't she mention my name in the live? I don't care how much love you so called got for someone, if they fucked you over that bad, any love one has for that person is dead. Instead, she told her true few that she was going to make a live about me, so they could tune in.

Anybody that was done wrong wouldn't care about putting someone on blast, right? They wouldn't speak indirectly, right? Everyone kept saying how grimy I was and how I owed her all of my loyalty, but that's bull crap because I was loyal until she pushed me away. There's a difference between loyalty and blind loyalty.

I could be grimy as ever and put the actual truth on Facebook about the things she's told me about the very people she's cool with and that's riding her wave. I could be grimy as ever and put her personal business out on Facebook, and I guarantee it would be one hell of a show, but that's not how I rock, regardless of what anyone thinks.

I couldn't understand why they would tell me all their business, cause fake beef, try to publicly shame me, and then make me an enemy. That was stupid. The tongue is a powerful tool. Do unto others as you would have them do unto you and understand that what goes around comes right back around.

Only, I'm not a vindictive person. I could have easily contacted every person that had something to say and told them what was said about them family and all, but I didn't and, no, it wasn't because I was afraid that she would tell them what I said because I gave zero fucks because if they came to me, I would tell them IF I did say anything. There's no bitch in my blood. A bitch bleeds just like me. Words are just that, words. People are going to talk about me until the day I die. Talk is cheap. It takes too much energy to be negative. Why give Facebook a show? I'm glad people think I'm scared. I'm glad people think I'm a punk ass bitch. I'm glad people think I won't bust a grape in a fruit fight. That's the exact thing I want people to think.

I was every fat, fake, homeless bitch in the book, but I didn't trip. I've grown so much that I'm going to let my silence be my response because sometimes, the best reaction is no reaction at all.

I remember losing everything, living out of trash bags, sleeping with my mother in her car, sleeping in roach infested hotels, and getting thrown out of those same hotels. I remember staying with my aunt and her forcing me to take cold showers because I wanted to sleep. I remember she would steal my clothes, and I went to school stinking because I had the same pair of panties on for a week. I remember watching my mother be ridiculed and disrespected by just about everyone.

I remember when I was on the road to self-publishing. I remember being able to afford any and everything I wanted. I remember looking in my bank account and seeing fifteen cents. I remember sending pussy pictures to a guy just to get money, so my nieces and nephews would have a beautiful Christmas.

I remember begging graphic designers for covers, trying to get on payment plans because I was BROKE. Crying to people who were supposed to be my friends, but they helped, just to talk about me afterwards. Yea, they were right. I was broke. Yea, they were right. I was homeless. Yea, they were right. I was begging for help. Yea, they were right. I borrowed money and wasn't sure when I would be able to pay it back.

You never know how strong you are until you lose EVERYTHING. You never know how strong you are until you hit underneath the bottom of the barrel. You never know how mature you are when you just no longer care to entertain negative things.

People can call me FAT. People can call me FAKE. People can call me BROKE. People can call me HOMELESS. People can call me WEAK. People call me WHATEVER they feel, I'm built Ford tough.

I never been ashamed of where I came FROM. Where I was AT. Where I am NOW, and where I'm GOING.

IF you're looking for the REDS JOHNSON that's going to be negative, you can forget that. If you're looking for the REDS JOHNSON that's going to see a post about her and she's going to respond, you can forget that. If you're looking for the REDS JOHNSON that's going to care how you feel about her, you can forget that.

Bitterness dims light, and my light will not be dimmed.

I know people like yo, she said so much shit about you, and you not going to say anything? Yes, she did have so much to say on live, but it was everything except for the truth. Like, at the time, I truly wished people took the time out to think, instead of assume. Why would a person let go of five years of friendship if something deep didn't happen? Why would a person completely shut down from someone who was so called genuinely there for them? Why would I leave an actual bed and go back to Jersey to sleep on a roach infested couch if something deep didn't happen?

People literally hate me so bad that they don't care to find out the facts. People love drama and they dwell on negativity too much and that results into them never knowing or wanting to know all the facts to a situation. In order for Aniya to feel good about herself, she had to make me look bad. She knew that people didn't fuck with me in the industry, so she knew that downing me on Facebook would work out in her favor. She knew that I wasn't going to respond on Facebook because people were just waiting for me to fuck up my career even more. She had to put the blame on me so that she would no longer feel guilty for messing up yet another friendship.

My mother Maria reached out to Aniya. Not because I asked because I didn't, but because my mother had been receiving messages as well.

"No, you sit back and keep writing. I'm going to handle this. Yea, you grown, but Aniya is almost my age and I'm not having this shit at all."

When my mother called Aniya, she told my mother she had to call her back and, when she did, she had her sister Asia and her mother Sonya on the phone with her. Why? I have no clue. My mother asked her what the problem was, and she said she reached her boiling point because people was coming back telling her stuff I said about her.

Now, I was told that in the live, Aniya made it clear that nobody liked me but, in the same token, you say that I was going back telling people stuff about you? How is that possible? If no one likes me or fucks with me, why would anyone listen to me about anything?

She said how I thought by putting all of my business on Facebook, it would stop people from coming for me, and that's a stupid scenario. I put my business out because I just don't give a fuck. I put my business out because I want to help someone who is afraid to tell their story. I put my business out because I own my flaws before someone else does. I put my business out because I want to inspire someone. I don't give a fuck if I put this book out and everyone gives me one stars. If I can touch just at least one person, then my job is done.

She also said how readers, authors, and publishers deleted her daily because of me, and how they were coming back to her telling her I said stuff about her. How much sense does that make? I'm not even a people person, and I'm picky with who I associate myself with. So, I'm risking my career by going to readers, publishers, and authors to talk about you? How much sense does that actually make?

She also told my mother how I hurt her because I stopped talking to her and that she was scared that I was going to put her business in my memoir because she saw me posting excerpts of my memoir and posting screenshots of the publishers that did me dirty. She was scared because I knew a lot about her, which was why she snapped the way that she did.

When my mother called me, all I could do was roll my eyes at the entire conversation. It was all a cop out, and I didn't care about it one bit. Apparently, she deleted the live and then went on Shyanna's status saying my peoples begged her to delete it, which was a complete lie. Everything she did was for show because she was angry and she had no way of getting to me. I wasn't answering her calls, texts, or inboxes. I wasn't supporting her like I used to, and I was doing my own thing. So, she had to find a way to break me or at least try to, and that's okay. People got to do what they got to do in order to stay relevant.

And not that I need to clarify anything because I don't care who believes her and who doesn't believe me but, for those who are wondering, no, I never talked about her family. If that was the case, wouldn't they have put me out? Wouldn't someone have come to Jersey to fight me? Wouldn't someone have called me and asked me what the problem was? Wouldn't there be proof of me speaking so bad about her family? Better yet, wouldn't Aniya have fought me, IF I spoke so badly about her family? People loved jumping on the 'I hate Reds Johnson' bandwagon, so it was to be expected to see so much hate and not enough common sense. No one was there to experience what I experienced, so for people to give input on a one-sided situation was immature and pointless, but people were going to be people.

However, like I stated before, no names were mentioned in the live, but people knew who she was talking about. After it was all said and done, I had to laugh like damn, little old me had you that bothered that I stopped talking to you that you had to do an hour live kicking my back in and it was lies at that? I'm loud, my name already been in too much shit, and people don't like me so, of course, she would plead to the people she knew didn't fuck with me. She had to make me look bad. She wanted to make me look bad so that no one will question her character once I revealed what had really gone down. Did it work? To her, it did because everyone agreed with her but, to me, it didn't. I'm still me, I'm still writing, I'm still pushing to achieve greatness, and I still don't give a damn who feels what towards me.

Do I care that Aniya is hurt or bothered that I stopped talking to her? Nope. Do I care about how people view me? Nope. Do I care that people think I'm a fake ass fat bitch? Nope. Do I care about how things played out? I dislike how messy things got but, nope, I don't care enough for it to bother me that much. It takes too much time and energy to dwell or focus on things I cannot change.

I don't care and I won't care. I had been team Aniya for too long and, now that I'm team Reds Johnson, she hates it. It eats her up inside how I slowly but surely bounced back. She wanted me to be stuck up her ass and ride her wave. She enjoyed me being her shadow for all those years. She enjoyed bragging about the many connections she had and how she couldn't take me along because of my attitude or my book titles. She enjoyed me not knowing my worth or potential. She enjoyed dumbing me down, and she enjoyed making me feel like I was less than her.

No, she never said any of those things. If I or anyone was to ask her if that's how she felt about Reds Johnson, she would deny it until her face turned blue, but I go by actions. I go by the way she treated me. I go by the things she's said to me and how she's said it to them. Aniya was the type of friend that wanted me to do good, just not better than her. For years, I've went by the words of people but, the moment I started going by actions, the true colors of people were quickly revealed.

I learned that in life, no matter how long you've known someone, if they become toxic, don't hesitate to get rid of them. That's what I did because the most dangerous person on earth is a fake friend. I had been friends with Aniya for almost five years and, in the end, I realized the entire time that I had been keeping the enemy close.

So, take a moment to think. If I can tell my life story. Speak on the many STD's I caught. Speak on how my pussy was stinking due to STD's, and even due to me wearing the same underwear for a week. Speak on how my father was on coke, and he was an alcoholic. Speak on how he beat my mother. Speak on how my mother was beat to a bloody pulp. Speak on how my siblings sexually and mentally abused me. Speak on how I paid a guy to be with me. Speak on the many sex partners I had. Speak on me attempting suicide and many other things. Why on earth would I lie about the things that took place during our friendship? I'm so disliked by people that everything I do bothers them. Everything they hear about me bothers them. The good they hear about me will be questioned, but the bad they hear about me won't be questioned. But, that's okay, I don't mind being disliked or even hated. I'll rather be disliked for being real, rather than being liked for being fake. Everyone that came into my life is either a lesson or a blessing, and she was my lesson.

68

Owning My Flaws: Finding My Purpose

For years, I downed myself for people walking out of my life. Whenever a man didn't want me, I thought that it was me that wasn't good enough. I felt like I needed to lose weight, so I would throw up everything I ate, or I would starve myself. I felt like I needed to be light skinned for me to be pretty, so I made sure to avoid the sun as much as I could. When I had a falling out with a family member, I tried to figure out what it was that I did wrong. Whenever I lost a friend, I figured it was something I did wrong.

But, after downing myself so much, I realized that I placed my power and my self-esteem in the hands of others. A person won't realize their potential or purpose if they're broken. They won't believe in themselves. My potential scared people. I had a certain light in me that people couldn't handle. It was the "I'm afraid of what she could become" fear.

I realized people envied me because I exposed myself before they could. When people live a life full of lies, it angers them to see someone else be so honest about things they wish they could be honest about. They envied me because regardless of how much I was talked about, I didn't fold. I went from nothing to something, then back to nothing, and now I have so much more. They envied me because no matter how many times people told me to shut the fuck up about what I been through, I still kept telling my story.

It wasn't me, it was the thought of me being great. It was my honesty, my realness, my courage.

People dislike me because of my strength and the fact that I live in my truth. I want people to see me flaws and all. I want people to know what it was like when I was at my worse. I want people to know the pain I felt when the people I trusted the most gave up on me. I'm not afraid to put myself on front street. I don't do this shit for likes. I do it because someone has to tell the story.

So, if anyone reading this feels the need to try and blast me on Facebook because you feel like I'm fake or I'm wrong for writing my truth, then by all means do what you must do. I'm done defending what doesn't need to be defended. What's understood doesn't need to be explained. I said what I had to say, and this will be the end of it.

Words is words, and I'll allow them to be just that; just as long as no one puts their hands on me, I'm good. People know that my career has been up and down and that if I do or say too much on Facebook, it will make me look bad, not them.

69

Love Me or Hate Me: I Am Her, She Is Me, I Am Reds Johnsn

LIFE WASN'T EASY FOR ME BY FAR. EVERY GUY I HAD RUN into used me and abused me sexually, mentally, physically, and emotionally. My family members disowned me because I was the mouthy one that spoke the truth and because I defended my mother. I had three older sisters that didn't give the slightest fuck about me. I had female friends who rather see me broken than successful, and I had a career that stressed me out something serious.

I suffered from depression, anxiety, and low-self-esteem. Throughout the years, I allowed men to use me and abuse me, which resulted in me sleeping with about twenty guys, hoping that at least one of them would end up genuinely liking me, but they didn't. So, I lived with that burden for years, knowing that I had given up my goods which was supposed to be my temple.

Writing this book brought so many emotions to the forefront. I cried, got angry, got sad, and sometimes depressed, but I kept pushing and I kept typing. It has brought such a relief for me to write this book and finally let out my pains, my hurt, my frustrations, and my truth. I done been close to death one too many times, so I had no choice but to start living.

Finally, I can speak without someone talking over me and, finally, I can speak without being told to humble myself, when all I was trying to do was tell my story. However, I did it, and this book will forever allow my story to be told.

I'm telling my story because for years, I've been angry, hurt, upset confused, and unhappy. My molestation confused me. My raped tore me apart. The many men I've slept with and encountered mentally tore me down. The many females I've befriended that betrayed me hurt my soul. I wasn't close to God like I should have been, but I prayed as best as I knew how. I prayed for guidance, but I felt like I was still at a standstill. I wanted to be happy, but I didn't know how. I didn't know the first thing about being happy.

I never understood my purpose in life. I never understood why I had to endure so much hurt, so much pain, so many struggles. I never understood why me? Then, I realized I needed to tell my story. I needed to see my pain and my struggles in words. It was me that needed to live my best life and help someone by telling my story.

So, here I am, I'm telling it. It wasn't easy. It wasn't a walk in the park. At times, I didn't even think I would make it. But, here I am, almost twenty-five years old and I'm still standing. My career is back like it never left. I have been blessed with my own home that I'll soon be moving in to. I'm working towards getting my GED, building my credit, and I'm changing the literary industry one book at a time.

I had been so angry for so many years. I had been so bitter for so many years. I had been so hurt for so many years that I just grew tired. Tired of fighting, tired of arguing, tired of hurting myself, and tired of that dark cloud that was following me everywhere I went.

Forgiving is something I never been good at. But, I can honestly say life goes on, and I forgive each and every one of you that has hurt me and that has caused me a great deal of pain. I forgive myself for allowing certain things to happen, and I forgive myself for carrying such a burden for so many years. I forgive myself for my hurt turning into anger, and I forgive myself for hindering myself from greatness. I may not have the high school education everyone wanted me to have. But, I'm an author. I went from nothing to having everything and then some.

I may be big, but I'm beautiful. I may be dark skinned, but my melanin is popping, and I'm beautiful. I may have a gapped tooth smile, but it's beautiful. I may have a tummy and stretch marks, but I'm sexy and I rock it well. I may have been bent in more ways than possible, but I was never broken. I thought I was, but the little bruises I did have was curable. The molestation, it didn't break me. The rape, it didn't break me. The bullying, it didn't break me. The suicide attempts, it didn't break me. The cheating, lying, and abuse men took me through, it didn't break me. The backstabbing friends I had, it didn't break me. The struggle, didn't break me. The tears, didn't break me. It molded me into being one hell of a woman I am today.

So, the question to those who tried to break me. I bet you didn't think this fat bitch would turn into a black Queen, did you?

My Voice, My Pain, My Truth

I AM

R J

Reds   Johnson

THE AUTHOR

Reds Johnson also known as Anne Marie, is a twenty-three-year-old independent author born and raised in New Jersey. She started writing at the age of nine years old, and ever since then, writing has been her passion. Her inspirations were Danielle Santiago, and Wahida Clark. Once she came across their books; Reds pushed to get discovered around the age of thirteen going on fourteen.

To be such a young woman, the stories she wrote hit so close to home for many. She writes urban, romance, erotica, bbw, and teen stories and each book she penned is based on true events; whether she's been through it or witnessed it. After being homeless and watching her mother struggle for many years, Reds knew that it was time to strive harder. Her passion seeped through her pores so she knew that it was only a matter of time before someone gave her a chance.

Leaping head first into the industry and making more than a few mistakes; Reds now has the ability to take control of her writing career. She is on a new path to success and is aiming for bigger and better opportunities.

Visit my website www.iamredsjohnson.com

MORE TITLES BY REDS JOHNSON

SILVER PLATTER HOE 6 BOOK SERIES

HARMONY & CHAOS 6 BOOK SERIES

OTHER TITLES BY REDS JOHNSON

CPSIA information can be obtained
at www.ICGtesting.com
Printed in the USA
LVHW081329141019
634138LV00016B/385/P